The Secret Of Imagination: Imagination Fulfills Itself

12 Lectures On The Creative Power of Imagination
From The World's Greatest Mystic

Neville Goddard

Compiled & Edited
by
David Allen

Copyright © 2021

Copyright © 2021 by Shanon Allen / David Allen

All rights reserved. No part of this publication may be reproduced, distributed, or transmitted in any form or by any means, including photocopying, recording, or other electronic or mechanical methods, without the prior written permission of the publisher, except in the case of brief quotations embodied in critical reviews and certain other noncommercial uses permitted by copyright law.
Printed in the United States of America

First Printing, May 2021

ISBN: 978-1-7370946-1-6

Published
by
Shanon Allen
Copyright © 2021

Introduction

Imagination Is Your Creative Power.

"The imaginative man does not deny the reality of the sensuous outer world of Becoming, but he knows that it is the inner world of continuous Imagination that is the force by which the sensuous outer world of Becoming is brought to pass." - Neville Goddard

I say to everyone: the whole vast world is now in your human imagination, and you can bring any desire out of it by believing it into being. First, you must know what you want, then create an image that fulfills it. Would your friends know and talk about it? Imagine they are with you now, discussing your fulfilled desire. You could be at a cocktail or dinner party that is being given in your honor. Or maybe it's a little get-together over tea. Create a scene in your mind's eye and believe its reality in! That invisible state will produce the objective state you desire, for all objective reality is solely produced by imagination. - Neville Goddard

Can you imagine a state and feel that your imaginal act is now a fact? It costs you nothing to imagine; in fact you are imagining every moment in time, but not consciously. But, may I tell you: if you use your creative power by imagining a desire is already fulfilled, when you get it, the circumstances will seem so natural that it will be easy to deny your imagination had anything to do with it, and you could easily believe that it would have happened anyway. But if you do, you will have returned to sleep once again. - Neville Goddard

Imagination is the creative power which can cause that which was not, to be! It can also cause that which is, not to be; therefore, it not only creates, but un-creates. - Neville Goddard

Imagination is the Cause of the Phenomena of Life

The Lectures

Lecture 1 .... Pages 7 - 11
Neville Goddard
By Imagination We Become
Radio Talk, Station KECA, Los Angeles
July, 1951

Lecture 2 .... Pages 12 - 23
Neville Goddard
Awakened Imagination
1954

Lecture 3 .... Pages 24 - 31
Neville Goddard
The Foundation Stone - Imagination
12-1-1959

Lecture 4 .... Pages 32 - 42
Neville Goddard
Is Christ Your Imagination
03-22-1963

Lecture 5 .... Pages 43 - 54
Neville Goddard
Imagination, My Slave
2-13-1967

Lecture 6 .... Pages 55 - 63
Neville Goddard
Imagining Creates
6-3-1968

Lecture 7 .... Pages 64 - 73
Neville Goddard
Imagination Fulfills Itself
10-26-1968

Lecture 8 ....Pages 74 - 81
Neville Goddard
The Perfect Image
04-11-1969

Lecture 9 ....Pages 82 - 107
Neville Goddard
Imagination
7-14-1969

Lecture 10 ....Pages 108 - 125
Neville Goddard
Secret of Imagination
6-21-1971

Lecture 11 ....Pages 126 - 133
Neville Goddard
How To Use Your Imagination
1955

Lecture 12 ....Pages 134 - 149
Neville Goddard
The Secret of Imagining
7-20-1970

Metaphysical Books By David Allen ....Pages 150 - 151

Lecture 1
Neville Goddard
By Imagination We Become
Radio Talk, Station KECA, Los Angeles
July, 1951

How many times have we heard someone say, "Oh, it's only his imagination?"

Only his imagination – man's imagination is the man himself. No man has too little imagination, but few men have disciplined their imagination. Imagination is itself indestructible. Therein lies the horror of its misuse. Daily, we pass some stranger on the street and observe him muttering to himself, carrying on an imaginary argument with one not present. He is arguing with vehemence, with fear or with hatred, not realizing that he is setting in motion, by his imagination, an unpleasant event which he will presently encounter.

The world, as imagination sees it, is the real world. Not facts, but figments of the imagination, shape our daily lives. It is the exact and literal minded who live in a fictitious world. Only imagination can restore the Eden from which experience has driven us out. Imagination is the sense by which we perceived the above, the power by which we resolve vision into being. Every stage of man's progress is made by the exercise of the imagination.

It is only because men do not perfectly imagine and believe that their results are sometimes uncertain, when they might always be perfectly certain. Determined imagination is the beginning of all successful operation. The imagination, alone, is the means of fulfilling the intention. The man who, at will, can call up whatever image he pleases is, by virtue of the power of his imagination, least of all subject to caprice. The solitary or captive can, by intensity of imagination and feeling, affect myriads so that he can act through many men and speak through many voices.

"We should never be certain", wrote William Butler Yeats in his IDEAS OF GOOD AND EVIL, "that it was not some woman treading in the winepress who began that subtle change in men's minds, or that the passion did not begin in the mind of some shepherd boy, lighting up his eyes for a moment before it ran upon its way."

Let me tell you the story of a very dear friend of mine, at the time the costume designer of the Music Hall in New York. She told me, one day, of her difficulty in working with one of the producers who invariably criticized and rejected her best work unjustly; that he was often rude and seemed deliberately unfair to her.

Upon hearing her story, I reminded her, as I am reminding you, that men can only echo to us that which we whisper to them in secret. I had no doubt but that she silently argued with the producer, not in the flesh, but in quiet moments to herself. She confessed that she did just that each morning as she walked to work. I asked her to change her attitude toward him, to assume that he was congratulating her on her fine designs and she, in turn, was thanking him for his praise and kindness. This young designer took my advice and, as she walked to the theater, she imagined a perfect relationship of the producer praising her work and she, in turn, responding with gratitude for his appreciation.

This she did morning after morning and in a very short while, she discovered for herself that her own attitude determined the scenery of her existence. The behavior of the producer completely reversed itself. He became the most pleasant professional employer she had encountered. His behavior merely echoed the changes that she had whispered within herself. What she did was by the power of imagination. Her fantasy led his; and she, herself, dictated to him the discourse they eventually had together at the time she was seemingly walking alone.

Let us set ourselves, here and now, a daily exercise of controlling and disciplining our imagination. What finer beginning than to imagine better than the best we know for a friend. There is no coal of character so dead that it will not glow and flame if but slightly turned.

The Secret Of Imagination: Imagination Fulfills Itself

Don't blame; only resolve. Life, like music, can, by a new setting, turn all its discords into harmonies. Represent your friend to yourself as already expressing that which he desires to be. Let us know that with whatever attitude we approach another, a similar attitude approaches us.

How can we do this? Do what my friend did. To establish rapport, call your friend mentally. Focus your attention on him and mentally call his name just as you would to attract his attention were you to see him on the street. Imagine that he has answered, mentally hear his voice – imagine that he is telling you of the great good you have desired for him. You, in turn, tell him of your joy in witnessing his good fortune. Having mentally heard that which you wanted to hear, having thrilled to the news heard, go about your daily task.

Your imagined conversation must awaken what it affirmed; the acceptance of the end wills the means. And the wisest reflection could not devise more effective means than those which are willed by the acceptance of the end. However, your conversation with your friend must be in a manner which does not express the slightest doubt as to the truth of what you imagine that you hear and say. If you do not control your imagination, you will find that you are hearing and saying all that you formerly heard and said.

We are creatures of habit; and habit, though not law, acts like the most compelling law in the world. With this knowledge of the power of imagination, be as the disciplined man and transform your world by imagining and feeling only what is lovely and of good report. The beautiful idea you awaken in yourself shall not fail to arouse its affinity in others. Do not wait four months for the harvest. Today is the day to practice the control and discipline of your imagination. Man is only limited by weakness of attention and poverty of imagination. The great secret is a controlled imagination and a well sustained attention, firmly and repeatedly focused on the object to be accomplished.

"Now is the acceptable time to give beauty for ashes, joy for mourning, praise for the spirit of heaviness; that they might be called trees of righteousness, the planting of the Lord that He might be glorified."

Now is the time to control our imagination and attention. By control, I do not mean restraint by will power, but rather cultivation through love and compassion. With so much of the world in discord, we cannot possibly emphasize too strongly the power of imaginative love.

Imaginative Love, that is my subject next Sunday morning, when I shall speak for Dr. Bailes, while he is on his holiday. The services will be held, as always, at the Fox Wilshire Theater, on Wilshire Boulevard, near La Cienega, at 10:30.

"As the world is, so is the individual", should be changed to, "As the individual is, so is the world".

And I hope to be able to bring to each of you present the true meaning of the words of Zechariah, "Speak ye every man the truth to his neighbor and let none of you imagine evil in your hearts against his neighbor"

What a wonderful challenge to you and to me.

"As a man thinketh in his heart, so is he."

As a man imagines, so is he. Hold fast to love in your imagination. By creating an ideal within your mental sphere, you can approximate yourself to this "ideal image" till you become one and the same with it, thereby transforming yourself into it, or rather, absorbing its qualities into the very core of your being. Never, never, lose sight of the power that is within you. Imaginative love lifts the invisible into sight and gives us water in the desert. It builds for the soul its only fit abiding place.

Beauty, love and all of good report are the garden, but imaginative love is the way into the garden.

Sow an imaginary conversation, you reap an act; Sow an act, you reap a habit; Sow a habit, you reap a character; Sow a character, you reap your destiny.

By imagination, we are all reaping our destinies, whether they be good, bad, or indifferent.

Imagination has full power of objective realization and every stage of man's progress or regression is made by the exercise of imagination. I believe, with William Blake, "What seems to be, is, to those to whom it seems to be, and is productive of the most dreadful consequences to those to whom it seems to be, even of torments, despair, and eternal death".

By imagination and desire, we become what we desire to be. Let us affirm to ourselves that we are what we imagine. If we persist in the assumption that we are what we wish to be, we will become transformed into that which we have imagined ourselves to be. We were born by a natural miracle of love and, for a brief space of time, our needs were all another's care. In that simple truth lies the secret of life. Except by love, we cannot truly live at all.

Our parents, in their separate individualities, have no power to transmit life. So, back we come to the basic truth that life is the offspring of love. Therefore, no love, no life.

Thus, it is rational to say that "God is Love". Love is our birthright. Love is the fundamental necessity of our life.

Do not go seeking for that which you are. Those who go seeking for love only make manifest their own lovelessness and the loveless never find love. Only the loving find love and they never have to seek for it.

Lecture 2
Neville Goddard
Awakened Imagination
1954

As you have heard, this morning's subject is "Awakened Imagination". It is my theme for the entire series of nineteen lectures. Everything is geared towards the awakening of the imagination. I doubt if there is any subject on which clear thinking is more rare than the imagination. The word itself is made to serve all kinds of ideas, many of them directly opposed to one another. But here this morning I hope to convince you that this is the redeeming power in man. This is the power spoken of in the Bible as the Second Man. "the Lord from Heaven".

This is the same power personified for us as a man called Christ Jesus.

In the ancient text it was called Jacob, and there are numberless names in the Bible all leading up and culminating in the grand flower called Christ Jesus. It may startle you to identify the central figure of the Gospels as human imagination, but I am quite sure before the series is over, you will be convinced that this what the ancients intended that we should know, but man has misread the Gospels as history and biography and cosmology, and so completely has gone asleep as to the power within himself.

Now this morning I have brought you the means by which this mighty power in us may be awakened.

I call it the art of revision. I take my day and I review it in my mind's eye. I start with the first incident in the morning. I go through the day; when I come to any scene in my unfolding day that displeased me, or if it didn't displease me if it was not as perfect as I thought it could have been, I stop right there and I revise it. I re-write it, and after I have re-written it so that it conforms to the ideal I wished I had experienced, then I experience that in my imagination as though I had experienced it in the flesh. I do it over and over until it takes on the tone of reality, and experience convinces me that that moment that I have revised and relived will not recede into my past.

It will advance into my future to confront me as I have revised it. If I do not revise it, these moments, because they never recede and they always advance, will advance to confront me perpetuating that strange, unlovely incident.

But if I refuse to allow the sun to descend upon my wrath, so that at the end of a day I never accept as final the facts of the day, no matter how factual they are, I never accept them, and revising it I repeal the day and bring about corresponding changes in my outer world.

Now, not only will this art of revision accomplish my every objective, but as I begin to revise the day it fulfills its great purpose and its great purpose is to awaken in me the being that men call Christ Jesus, that I call my wonderful human imagination, and when it awakens it is the eye of God and it turns inward into the world of thought and there I see that what formerly I believed to exist on the outside really exists within myself.

No matter what it is, I then discover that the whole of Creation is rooted in me and ends in me as I am rooted in and end in God. And from that moment on I find my real purpose in life and my real purpose is simply to do the will of Him that sent me, and the will of Him that sent me is this – that of all that he has given me I shall lose nothing but raise it up again.

And what did he give me? He gave me every experience in my life. He gave me you. Every man, woman and child that I meet is a gift to me from my Father, but they fell in me because of my attitude towards society, because of my attitude towards myself.

When I begin to awaken and the eye opens and I see the whole is myself made visible, I then must fulfill my real purpose, which is the will of Him that sent me, and the Will is to raise up those that I allowed in my ignorance when I slept to descend within me.

The Secret Of Imagination: Imagination Fulfills Itself

Then starts the real art of revision; to be the man, regardless of your impressions of that man, regardless of the facts of the case that are all staring you in the face, it is your duty when you become awakened to lift him up within yourself and you will discover that he was never the cause of your displeasure. When you look at him and you are displeased, look within and you will find the source of the displeasure. It did not originate there.

Now let me give you a case history to illustrate this point. I know a few of you were at the banquet and maybe a few of you heard me last Thursday on T.V. but I doubt in this audience of say twenty-three or twenty-four hundred of us, that more than say a hundred and fifty heard it, and even if you heard it you can hear it time and time again for it is this, that if you hear it will cause you to act upon it because as I told you, and I think I did last Sunday, but if I didn't let me tell you now; if you attended the entire nineteen and you became saturated with all that I have to tell you, so that you had all the knowledge you think it takes to achieve your objectives, and you did not apply what you received, it would avail you nothing; but a little knowledge which you carry out in action, you will find to be far more profitable than much knowledge which you neglect to carry out in action. So by repeating this case history this morning, though say a hundred or two hundred of you have heard it, it will help you to remember you must do something about it.

This past May in New York City, there sat a lady who had been coming for years and I made a simple observation that people must become doers of the word and not mere hearers only.

For if a man only hears it and never applies what he hears he will never really prove or disprove what he has heard; and then I told the story of a lady who had only heard me three or four times and how she transformed the life of another, and this lady hearing what one who came only three times and this miracle took place in her life, she went home determined that she would really apply what she had heard over the years, and this is what she did.

The Secret Of Imagination: Imagination Fulfills Itself

Two years before, after a violent quarrel, she was ordered out of her son's home by her daughter-in-law. Her son said "Mother, you need no proof from me that I love you: it's obvious: I think I have proven that every day of my life, but if that is Mary's decision, and I regret it, it must be my decision, for I love Mary and we live in the same house and it is our house: it is our little family, and I am sorry she feels this way about it, but you know these little things that culminate in an explosion as took place today. If that is her decision, it is mine". That was two years ago.

She went home and she realized that night after night for over two years she had allowed the sun to descend upon her wrath. She thought of this wonderful family that she loved and felt herself ostracized from it, expelled from the home of her son. She did nothing about revising it and yet I had been talking revision to my New York audience for the past year.

This is what she did now. She knew the morning's mail brought nothing. This was a Wednesday night. There had been no correspondence in two years. She had sent her grandson at least a dozen gifts in the two years. Not one was ever acknowledged. She knew they had been received for she had insured many of them; so she sat down that night and mentally wrote herself two letters – one from her daughter-in-law, expressing a great kindness for her, saying that she had been missed in the home and asking her when she was coming to see them; then she wrote one from her grandson in which he said "Grandmother, I love you". Then came a little expression of thanks for the last birthday present, which was in April, and then came a feeling of sadness rather because he hadn't seen her and begging her to come and see him soon.

These two short notes she memorized and then, as she was about to sleep, she took her imaginary hands and held these letters and she read them mentally to herself until they woke in her the feeling of joy because she had heard from her family; that she was wanted once more. She read these letters over and over feeling the joy that was hers because she had received them and fell asleep in her project. For seven nights this lady read these two letters. On the morning of the eighth day she received the letter: on the inside there were two letters – one from her grandson and one from her daughter-in-law. These letters were identical with the letters she had mentally written to herself seven days before.

Where was the estrangement? Where was the conflict? Where was the source of the displeasure that was like a running sore over two years? When man's eye is opened he realizes all that he beholds, though it appears without, it is within – within one's own imagination, of which this world of mortality is but a shadow.

She gave me permission to tell that story. When I told it, and we came to the period of questions and answers, there was a strange reaction from that crowd. They wondered what joy life would hold for any of us if we had to write our own letters; if we had to do everything to ourselves that seemingly is done in joy; that seemingly is spontaneous coming from another; but I don't want to write myself a love letter from my wife, or my sweetheart or my friend. I want that one to feel this way towards me and to express it unknown to me that I may receive a surprise in life.

Well, I am not denying that sleeping man firmly believes that is the way things happen. When a man awakes he realizes that everything he encounters is apart of himself, and what he does not now comprehend, he knows, because the eye is opened, that it is related by affinity to some as yet unrealized force in his own being; that he wrote it but he has forgotten it, that he slapped himself in the face but he has forgotten it; that within himself he started the entire unfolding drama, and he looks out upon a world, and it seems strange to him, because most of us in our sleep are totally unaware of what we are doing from within ourselves.

What that lady did, every man and woman in this audience today can do. It will not take you years to prove it; what I tell you now may startle you; it may seem to be bordering on insanity for the insane believe in the reality of subjective states and the sane man only believes in what the senses will allow, what they will dictate, and I'm going to tell you when you begin to awake, you assert the supremacy of imagination and you put all things in subjection to it.

You never again bow before the dictates of facts and accept life on the basis of the world without.

To you Truth is not confined by facts but by the intensity of your imagination.

So here we find the embodiment of Truth, which I say is human imagination, standing in the world drama before the embodiment of reason personified as Pontius Pilate. And he is given the authority to question truth and they ask him, "What is the truth?" and Truth remains silent. He refuses to justify any action of his; he refuses to justify anything that was done to him, for he knows no man cometh unto me save I call him: no man takes away my life, I lay it down myself.

You didn't choose me, I have chosen you. For here is Truth seeing nothing hereafter in pure objectivity, but seeing everything subjectively related to himself and he the source of all the actions that take place within his world; so Truth remains absolutely silent and says nothing when reason questions him concerning the true definition of Truth.

Because when the eye opens it knows that what is an idea to sleeping man is a fact to the awakened imagination, an objective fact, not an idea. I entertain the idea of a friend and I make some wonderful concept of him in my mind's eye and when I sleep it seems to be a wish, it seems to be the longing of my heart, but purely subjective, just an idea. And the eye within me opens, and he stands before me embodying the quality that I desired in my sleep to see him express. So what is an idea to sleeping man, the unawakened imagination, is an objective reality to awakened imagination.

Now, this exercise calls for, I would say, the active, voluntary use of imagination as against the passive, involuntary acceptance of appearances.

We never accept as true and as final anything unless it conforms to the ideal we desire to embody within our world, and we do exactly what the grandmother did. But now we start it and we do it daily. You may get your results tomorrow; it may come the day after; it may come in a week, but I assure you they will come. You do not need some strange laboratory, like our scientists, to prove or disprove this theory.

Here in 1905 a young man startled the scientific world with his equation that no one could even test. It is said not six men lived who could understand his equation. It was 14 years later before Lord Rutherford could devise the means to test that equation and he found that it was true, not 100%, because he did not have the means at his hand to really give it a complete test. It was another 14 years before further tests could be made. And you know the results of that equation that Einstein gave us in 1905. For today man, not knowing the power of his own imagination, stands startled at the results of that unlocking of energy. But he was the man who said, and I put it in the first page of my new book – "Imagination is more important than knowledge" That was Albert Einstein.

Imagination is more important than knowledge.

For if man accepts as final the facts that evidence bears witness to, he will never exercise this God-given means of redemption, which is his imagination. Now I'm going to ask you to test this: you will not take the three weeks that I am here to prove it or disprove it, but the knowledge of it cannot prove itself, only the application of that knowledge can prove it or disprove it. I know from experience you cannot disprove it.

Take an objective, take a job, take some conversation with your boss, take an increase in salary. You say well, the job doesn't allow it, or maybe the Union will not allow it. I don't care what doesn't allow it.

Yesterday morning's mail brought me one, where, in San Francisco, this captain, a pilot, and he writes me that I saw him backstage after one of my meetings, and there he said, "But Neville, you are up against a stone wall. I am a trained pilot; I have gone all over the world, all over the seven seas; I'm a good pilot and I love the sea, not a thing in this world I want to do but go to sea; yet they restrict me to certain waters because of seniority.

No matter what argument I give them the Union is adamant and they have closed the book on my request." I said, "I don't care what they have done, you are transferring the power that rightfully belongs to God, which is your own imagination, to the shadow you cast upon the screen of space.

"So here, we are in this room; need it remain a room? Can't you use your imagination to call this a bridge.

This is now a bridge and I am a guest on the bridge of your ship, and you are not in waters restricted by the Union; you are in waters that you desire to sail your ship. Now close your eyes and feel the rhythm of the ocean and feel with me and commune with me and tell me of your joy in first proving this principle. and secondly in being at sea where you want to be.

He is now in Vancouver on a ship bringing a load of lumber down to Panama. He has a complete list that will take him through the year what this man has to do. He is going into waters legitimately that the Union said he could not go. This doesn't dispense with unions, but it does not put anyone in our place – no one, kings, queens, presidents, generals, we take no one and enthrone him and put him beyond the power that rightfully belongs to God. So I will not violate the law but things will open that I will never devise.

I will sit in the silence and within myself I will revise the picture. I will hear the very man who told me "No, and that's final" and hear him tell me yes, and a door opens. I don't have to go and pull strings or pull any wires whatsoever.

I call upon this wonderful power within myself, which man has forgotten completely because he personified it and called it another man, even though it is a glorious picture of a man but that is not the man: the real man is not in some other world.

When religion speaks, if it's a real religion, it speaks not of another world; it speaks of another man that is latent but unborn in every man that has attunement with another world of meaning, so that man sat and he tuned in with another world of meaning and brought into being a power that he allowed to go to sleep because he read the laws of man too well.

He accepted as final the dictate of facts for they read him the by-laws, they read him the laws of the Union.

And here today he is flying the ocean as he wants to do it.

The grandmother is no longer locked out from the home she loved, but she is in communion, but she was locked out by herself for two years. And he was locked out by himself for well over 18 months, and burning up day after day allowing the sun to descend upon his wrath when he had the power within himself and the key to unlock every door in the world.

I say to each and every one of you I wouldn't take from you your outer comfort, your religion, for all these things are like toys for sleeping man, but I come to awaken within you that which when it awakes it sees an entirely different world.

It sees a world that no man when he sleeps could ever see, and then he starts to raise within himself every being that God gave him; and may I tell you God gave you every man that walks the face of the earth. He also gave it for this purpose that nothing is to be discarded. Everyone in the world must be redeemed and your individual life is the process by which this redemption is brought to pass.

So we don't discard because the thing is unpleasant, we revise it; revising it we repeal it, and as we repeal it, it projects itself on the screen of space bearing witness to the power within us, which is our wonderful human imagination.

And I say human advisedly – some would have me say the word divine. The very word itself means nothing to man. He has pushed it off from himself completely and divorced himself from the thing that he now bows before and calls by other names. I say human imagination.

As Blake said "Rivers, mountains, cities, villages all are human". When the eye opens you see them in your own bosom, in your own wonderful bosom they all exist, they are rooted there. Don't let them fall and remain fallen; lift them up for the will of my Father is this, that of all that he has given me I should lose nothing but raise it up again, and I raise it up every time I revise my concept of another and make him conform to the ideal image I myself would like to express in this world. When I do unto him what I would love the world to do unto me, and see in me I am lifting him up.

And may I tell you what happens to that man when he does it? First of all, he is already turned around within himself. He no longer sees the world in pure objectivity, but the whole world subjectively related to himself, and hang it upon himself. As he lifts it up do you know he blooms within himself. When this eye of mine was first opened I beheld man as the prophet saw him. I saw him as a tree walking: some were only like little antlers of a stag, others were majestic in their foliage, and all that were really awake were in full bloom. These are the trees in the garden of God. As told us in the old ancient way of revision in the 61st chapter of the Book of Isaiah – "Go and give beauty for ashes, go and give joy for mourning, give the spirit of praise for the spirit of heaviness, that they may become trees of righteousness, plantings to the glory of God."

That is what every man must do, that's revision. I see ash when the business is gone; you can't redeem it, you can't lift it up, conditions are bad and the thing has turned to ash.

Put beauty in its place; see customers, healthy customers, healthy in finances, healthy in the attitude towards you, healthy in every sense of the word. See them loving to shop with you if you are a shopkeeper; if you are a factory worker, don't see anything laying you off, lift it up, put beauty in the place of ash, for that would be ash if you were laid off with a family to feed. If someone is mourning, put joy in the place of mourning; if someone is heavy of spirit, put the spirit of praise in place of the spirit of heaviness, and as you do this and revise the day you turn around, and turning around you turn up, and all the energies that went down when you were sound asleep and really blind now turn up and you become a tree of righteousness, a planting to the glory of God. For I have seen them walking this wonderful earth, which is really the Garden; we have shut ourselves out by our concept of self and we have turned down.

As told us in the Book of Daniel, we were once this glorious tree and it was felled to the very base, and what formerly sheltered the nations and fed the nations and comforted the bird and gave some comfort to the animals from the sun of the day, of the heat of the day; and suddenly some voice said from within, "Let it lie, let it remain as it is, but do not disturb the roots; I will water it with the dew of heaven and as I water it with the dew of heaven it will once more grow again, but this time it will consciously grow, it will know what it really is and who it is. In its past it was majestic but it had no conscious knowledge of its majesty, and I felled it – that was the descent of man. And now, he will once more spring from within himself and he will be a tree walking, a glorious, wonderful tree.

Now to those who are sound asleep this may seem to you too startling: this may be just as startling as Einstein's equation was; that was startling too. But I tell you I've seen it and I see it – men are destined to be trees in the garden of God. They are planted on earth for a purpose and they don't always remain men, they are transformed as they turn in and turn up. This is the true meaning of the transfiguration. There is a complete metamorphosis taking place like the grub into the butterfly. You don't remain what you appear to be when man is asleep, and there is no more glorious picture in the world than to see this living animated human being, for every branch within him is represented by an extension of himself called another, and when he lifts the other up that branch not only comes into leafage but it blossoms and the living human blossoms that blossom upon the tree of man who awakens.

So that's my message for you this year; I'll give it to you to stir into being that which sleeps in you, for the son of God sleeps in man and the only purpose of being is to awaken him. So it is not to awaken this, nice as it appears to be, but this man of sense – is only a casing: it is called the first man, but the first shall be last and the last shall be first. So that which comes into being second, like Jacob coming second from his mother's womb, he takes precedence over his brother Esau who came first. Esau was the one like this, he was made of skin and hair, and Jacob was made a smooth skinned lad, but that one that comes second suddenly becomes the lord of all the nations and that one sleeps in every man born of woman, and it is the duty of a teacher or a true religion to awaken that man, not to talk of another world, not to make promises to be fulfilled beyond the grave, but to tell him as he awakens now he is in heaven and the kingdom is come now, this day, on earth. For as he awakens he revises his day and he repeals his day and projects a more beautiful picture onto the screen of space.

Lecture 3
Neville Goddard
The Foundation Stone - Imagination
12-1-1959

We believe that man can create anything he desires.

We believe the Universe is infinite response and the one who causes it is the individual perceiver. Nothing is independent of your perception of it.

We are so interwoven we are part of the machine, but as we awake we detach ourselves from this machine and make life as we wish it to be.

"For man is all Imagination and God is man and exists in us and we in him." "The eternal body of man is the Imagination: that is God himself." You can imagine and I can imagine, and if we can be faithful to the state imagined it must appear in our world.

This is not new. This was given centuries ago, for we have it in the Bible; but people do not know how to read the Bible, so they got together and organized it into an "ism." It is not an "ism," but it is the great plan to free man.

The Bible shows this plan in detail.

We will turn to a few passages and show you what those who wrote it intended we should see.

Isaiah 28:16: "Thus says the Lord God, 'Behold, I am laying in Zion for a foundation a stone, a tested stone, a precious cornerstone, of a sure foundation: He who believes will not be in haste.'" Now, we are told in the Book of Psalms that the world rejected the stone. "The stone which the builders rejected has become the head of the corner." "You cannot lay any other stone." "On this stone you may build gold, silver, hay, or stubble and the day will reveal it." I tell you that this stone is your Imagination, and it is called in the Bible: Christ Jesus, or God, or the Lord. It is your Imagination, which is one with the Divine Imagination which created, sustains, changes, and even destroys parts of the creation. This is the stone that is tested and it is a sure foundation, and he who believes in it will not be in haste. If I can but imagine and know that imagining creates reality I will not be impatient or lead a superficial life. When a man does not live in his Imagination he will become impatient of the outcome of what he desires, and finally he will become violent in his effort to get things.

Here is one who asks the question: "Who do men say that the Son of Man is?" Some said this and some that, but again he asked: "But who do you say that I AM?" "And Simon Peter replied, 'You are the Christ, the Son of the Living God.' And Jesus answered him, 'Blessed are you, Simon Bar-Jona! For flesh and blood has not revealed this to you, but my Father who is in Heaven. And I tell you, you are Peter, and on this rock I will build my church."

The churches tell you that it means a man called Peter. It is not an individual. The whole thing takes place in the mind of you the individual. You imagine a certain state and it is called Peter. If it were a man called Peter, you would not find what you find six verses later. For there he turns to the same character, Peter, and says to him: "Get behind me Satan: You are a hindrance to me; for you are not on the side of God, but of men." That is what every man in the world does. He gets a revelation and he realizes the foundation stone is Imagining. He sees a friend who needs help and he imagines he has what he wants. If he believes it, he is not in haste. He is imagining what he wants and he is not violent, and he is not concerned, and he does not give suggestions to the friend as to what to do physically to bring his desire to pass. If the foundation stone is true, there is only one power to support it. If he knows that, he will not allow himself to be turned; he will remain faithful to his assumption. But we are told in the Bible story that the one who had been commended, Peter, turned and became violent, and then Jesus said to him, "Get behind me, Satan." You turn back to the ways of men to get things to go as you want them to go. You pull all the wires and therefore you have turned from the only foundation in the world, and that is Christ Jesus, which is human Imagination. If you believe this you will not reject the stone.

"Stone" is "even" [in Hebrew] and it means to create, or build, or beget children. Here is a stone in "Zion" (which means a high pinnacle or a barren place). That is man, before the stone is sunk in him. He is the waste, the desert. Sunk in man as his Imagination is the only foundation stone, for [there is] no other foundation of the living God and he has sunk himself in me. Therefore, I AM the son of the living God, for there is only one and I AM he. If I believe this, I will not be impatient. "He who believes it will not be in haste." This is the Lord's way. I ask you to test it. Bring before your mind's eye what you want to see in this world. It may be business or a friend's good fortune. It can be anything, for on this foundation you can put stubble, or wood, or hay. You are building with hay when you say of someone: "I know – he was no good." They lived in that state concerning another and then it came to pass – and they say: "I always thought he was like that." Some of us build strange things for another. We were imagining on the only foundation, but we have put stubble on it instead of gold or silver, and the day revealed it, and then we cannot relate what happens to anything we have done.

The Hebrew meaning of the "stone" is to beget children. All the events of my life are my children. Everyone can build on this one foundation. "I AM laying in Zion a stone." What stone? God is burying himself in everyone in the world. It is a true stone, a precious cornerstone, and one who believes will not be in haste. I have seen an imaginal act take two years to come forth, but when it appeared – what a giant! I have seen it come in an hour. But do not be in haste or think there is any other foundation and – like Peter – turn to another foundation, growing violent toward those who would lead Jesus to the cross. But Christ said: "I came to move toward the cross. Get behind me, Satan. You are a hindrance to me."

If I am still in the machine, I think the good things come only by accident or chance. Let the wheel turn, for each must go through all the furnaces until he awakens and sees the whole universe as infinite response. The day will come when every person, at a certain degree of awakening, will freeze an activity within himself, and as it comes to a stop within him, that whole section is "dead." The laws of nature are only free action, repeated until they become accepted as a law. Yet you will see leaves in mid-air not falling, and people moving in space will cease to move but will not fall, for as you stopped the action within yourself the whole thing stopped. And you will see the whole thing as Zion – the desert – and the only thing that makes it alive is the stone buried in it. But man becomes lost in the things he has made and gives to them the power. For example, through the use of his Imagination he brings money into his world; then he forgets that it was the activity of his mind that did this, and he sees in the money itself the power to get what he desires. But when he awakes he will no longer lose himself in his own creation.

I say to everyone here: there is only one stone. If tonight there is someone very ill who needs your help and you imagine the best for him and then you get news that he is worse tomorrow, do not be impatient, but remain faithful to the one stone laid in Zion. What more can you do after you have imagined? Someone writes to you about a problem. Imagine for them what they desire and then do not turn aside to do anything to make it come true. You remain faithful, and it will create the conditions necessary to bring fulfillment.

You can look at someone with deep concern and want a change. You do not voice it, but lock it in, and then forty-eight hours later there is initiated what you set in motion. And they wonder: "Could my problem be traced to so-and-so?" Just the very thing you had been thinking! You entertained their problem with deep concern, and then you will ask: "Did you influence me or did I influence you? When did you entertain this thought?" And they say: "Just now," and then you say: "Forty-eight hours ago I entertained this thought, but I did not say it aloud." That makes no difference. All things by a law divine in one another's beings mingle. We all influence each other. We are all interpenetrated, and the more one is deeply concerned for another, the more he is penetrated by another.

The Secret Of Imagination: Imagination Fulfills Itself

I say the universe is infinite response, but it also gives back more than you imagine. It is pressed down and running over. Therefore, to be negative can be frightening. The good will come back a thousand-fold, but so will the negative. But if I am optimistic and do not waver, I will bring that also pressed down and running over. It is something wonderful; it will come like a gusher. The world responds more than it takes, and it gives to the individual more than he imagines – good or bad.

I say to everyone that the greatest of books is the Bible, but people have organized it, and even say they have found the remains of Peter or some other Biblical character. Peter is not a man, but a state. You rise up to the crown of it all and that is Christ. States are permanent but I am not fixed; I am a living moving being. I can be praised for one state and then I see a morning headline, say, and move from that true foundation, and then the power rebukes me as Satan, for I reacted instead of acted. Would you like to be in the state called Peter, the one addressed in Matthew 16? How? Let me say, and mean it: "My Imagination is God and there is no other." It is one with the supreme power and let me live in that state, and then I am being addressed: "You are blessed, Simon Bar-Jona." It means the depth of my being is giving it to me. Can I do it? The day that you do it and remember you did it, at that moment you are relating that story. When Peter confessed: "Thou art the Christ," that is the stone on which the whole thing rests, but when he got away from that and reacted, then he was called Satan, or the re-actor.

God is begetting sons by means of the stone. He buries himself in every man in the world, but he is rejected. I can tell you these things here, but if I told them across the airways I would be immediately turned off. People cannot believe they are responsible for their imaginal acts. They do not want to believe it. I cannot be free of the results of what I imagine. Go out determined to prove it, and having proved it, keep the stone alive. There is no other stone. "No other can any man lay, which is Christ Jesus," But on this build anything – but build gold, do not build hay or stubble. I want everyone here to test it. Take someone who is really distressed, and if you believe in the foundation you will leave here tonight without any concern for them, even if you receive wires stating things are worse. It might take a week or a month, but that which you have imagined, if you remain faithful to the stone, will come.

I have seen a man looking at a building – which is an inanimate thing – and you would say it could not respond. How can he look at it and see his name on it when he does not have a nickel? But he did it. I know the man. [Neville's brother] and in a way he could not have devised, the building became his. Let no one tell you that something cannot respond, but when we are still part of the machine, we cannot quite see that we are the cause of everything in our world, and we hope good fortune will smile on us. Then when you set something bad in motion, as the machine turns you cannot see what caused it, but when you become awake you can control the machine. It responds to the imaginal acts of the awakened man, for the awakened man is in control.

A thrill is in store for you when you can finally stop all activity and the whole thing will freeze. You will know what the so-called wise men say, but you will hear only these words: "I thank you Father that you have hid these things from the wise and pious and revealed them unto babes." For you will know that it is the perceiver who is making everything alive. For you will find that nothing is independent of the mind of the perceiver. A truly awakened teacher could freeze certain sections for the edification of his students if he chose. By normal standards everything would die if you suspended activity; but it does not die, for there is nothing outside of your perception of it. Take your boss or an employee and represent them to yourself as you want them to be, and believe in the reality of the foundation stone, and then you will not make haste to bring it to pass. For Imagination is creating reality, and in a way no one knows it will be brought to pass if you remain faithful to that foundation stone. It makes no difference who you are or what you have. The man who cannot always sign a check to realize a dream is better off, for he is more awake; for he must use the talent God gave him, which is God himself. If I can always put pressure on someone to get what I want, I will never know I am this machine. But if I have to do it all within myself, then I know.

A story was told me tonight of a man who had lost his wife at the birth of his son, and the child was taken to St. Louis to be brought up by his wife's sister. This man had tried for seven years to get enough ahead to take a trip to St. Louis to see the child. He constantly tried to see himself getting a job with more money so he could make the trip. He was told that by the right use of this law he should only see himself with his child and let the way be left to God. Following this he was given a job that took him from Los Angeles to New Orleans. But that was not near St. Louis. He took the job and persisted in his dream, and in three months he was transferred to the St. Louis run and given a twenty-four hour layover there every week.

The best thing that ever happened to me was when I was fired from Macy's during the depression. I might be captain of the elevators if I had stayed there. My father lost everything he owned, and that proved to be the beginning of the great dream he brought to pass. One person believed in him and he started on that, and when he made his exit last October, he had given to his community much that no one had ever given before. The blackest day of his life turned out to be the bright day of his life. No matter what you have done, forget it. You are God and God is untarnished, for he is all imagining.

Now, you start to imagine and make it something of which you can be proud. Make it big. If it is truly the stone being laid in Zion, do not turn to any argument of man. You be faithful, and whatever you put on the stone as an imaginal activity will come into your world. Of course, you may go back to the world of men, like Peter. He denied the stone three times but he did then return to it again. You may do that, but in the end you will learn, for in the depth of your being the words are being said: "Get behind me, Satan." But I have seen people forget. I have seen them rise from nothing to great heights and then say: "It would have happened anyway." They do not believe that their imaginal activity was the foundation on which they built that structure. There is only one stone and that is your wonderful Imagination.

This works better if you do not try to aid it on the outside, for it is not flesh and blood that revealed it to you. You got it from the Christ.

Now let us go into the silence.

Lecture 4
Neville Goddard
Is Christ Your Imagination
03-22-1963

Tonight's subject is in the form of a question: "Is Christ your Imagination?" When we ask the question we expect the answer in terms of our current background of thought, and quite often that is not adequate to frame the answer. Now, I am asking the question, and in order to answer myself I should really clarify the terms, "imagination" and "Christ" I think there will be no problem tonight if I define – say – "imagination." I think you will agree with me when I define "Christ." If I say to that, that imagination is the power of performing mental images, you wouldn't quarrel with that. Sitting here tonight, you can think of anything and see it mentally. You may not see it as graphically as you see it in its present form in the room at the moment, but you could see it vividly in the mind's eye and discriminate. Think of a tree, a horse, and you know the difference between one and the other, and they are two separate objects in your mind's eye. Well, that is the power of imagination.

When it comes to Christ – and there are hundreds of millions in the world that call themselves Christians – the very use of the word instantly conjures in the mind's eye a person. They think of Christ as a person, and no two have the same mental picture of this person. I know, many, many years ago in New York City this French artist went to the library on 42nd street and brought up 46 different pictures of Christ and screened them with his little lantern. No two were alike, and each artist claimed that this was an inspired picture as it was presented to him, and he painted the picture. There were blond and blue-eyed pictures, dark swarthy skin; there were those with a very black skin – all 46 pictures were projected as so-called originals. So, man has been conditioned to believe that Christ is a person. So I ask the question: "Is Christ your imagination?" Can I personify the imagination? I will.

Let us go back to the Bible. What does the Bible say of Christ? In Paul's first letter to the Corinthians (I will just give you the highlights) he defines Christ as: "The power and the wisdom of God." In John 1 (which brings Christology to its height, as far as the Bible goes – there is no single book that takes the secret of Christ and brings it to this height as you will find in the Gospel of John) – in the Gospel of John, speaking now of this presence that was with God, his meaning, his power: "By Him all things were made and without Him was not anything made that was made." It is the power and yet it is wisdom. So here is a creative power. If I take that now and analyze myself in another world, the sign goes to the end of the second letter to the Corinthians. He calls upon all of us who would read that letter: "Test yourself. Do you not realize that Jesus Christ is in thee?"

Here we are told: "All things were made by Him." He is the power of God and the wisdom of God. Every attribute of God is personified. So his power is personified, and may I confess I have seen that power – and it is a man. I have seen that wisdom – and it is a man. And when you stand in the presence of that personified aspect of infinite being, you know you are standing in the presence of infinite might. It is not just power, it is almighty-ness, and you stand in the presence – and yet it is a man. So here he calls it the power and the wisdom.

Now he asks me, and you who read his letter, to test ourselves: "Test yourself, do you not realize that Jesus Christ is in thee." And he made all these things – well then, let us put him to the test in us. I say he is our imagination, that is the power, the creative power of the universe. Look around. Do you know anything in the world of man that man has created – from the clothes that he wears to the homes that he inhabits – that wasn't first imagined? Do you know of anything in this world that is now proved as fact, as a concrete reality, that wasn't first imagined – only imagined, and then it externalized? Yes, using hands, using implements of the world, but it first began as an image, and an image is simply the product of this reforming image-making faculty in man, which is man's imagination. Now, if "All things were made by him and without him was not anything made that was made," I can't come to any other conclusion than the fact that Christ of scripture is my imagination.

Now who is Jesus? If Christ is the power and the wisdom of God, and God sunk himself in us, that was his sacrifice. He actually became us that we may live; for were it not for this sacrifice of God, to actually limit himself to the state called "man," man would – like the earth – wear out like a garment. As we are told in Isaiah 51:6: "Lift up your eyes to the heavens, and look at the earth beneath; for the heavens will vanish like smoke, the earth will wear out like a garment, and they who dwell in it will do likewise; but my salvation will be forever and my deliverance will never be ended." That word "salvation" means Jesus. The word "Jesus" is "Jehovah saves." That is salvation. That is forever. Were it not that God became man that man may become God, to save man and lift him up to immortality, because the promise is: "The earth will wear out like a garment."

Our scientists tell us today that the sun is melting in radiation. If it took unnumbered billions of years, if it started a process of melting, no matter how long it takes it has an end, and with its end we have our end as part of the system. So we, walking the earth, always have an end. To stop that process of bringing man to an end: "My salvation will be forever and my deliverance will never have an end."

So, God became man that man may become God. In becoming man (as God is the only creative power in the world) what in me creates? My imagination. I may not have the talent to put it on paper, I may not have the ability to execute it the way artists can, but I can imagine it. I can imagine a book and the joy of having a book. I can imagine a picture. Without being an artist I can dream. I cannot conceive of a picture that a man can paint on canvas that is more alive than my dream, yet I can't put a thing on canvas. But I go to sleep and I can dream. And what is doing it, if not my imagination? And here when I lose the conscious faculty, this restricted area, I can actually dream. Dream as no artist in the world conveys; put color upon it, put motion upon it, and have the most wonderful drama – and that is my imagination.

But this is not the only power and wisdom of God. In the greatest of all the New Testament, which is John, John does not emphasize the power. He states in the beginning – yes, he declares might as power – but the emphasis is not on power; it is on redemption and revelation. Revelation in John's gospel is an act of God in self-revealing. So, in the first chapter he tells us what this power will do for us. First of all there are two endings to John. Let us take the real ending, which is the 20th chapter, the first ending, and whoever the writer is who calls himself John: "Now Jesus did many other signs that are not written in this book; but these are written that you may believe that Jesus is the Christ . . .and believing have life in his name." He is the power and the wisdom of God. That is what the author is telling us in the very end. Many signs he did, but in spite of the number of the signs and the character of the signs, it did not evoke faith. The whole teaching of the Gospel of John is based upon faith and unbelief in him. Either one or the other. Have faith in him, or you disbelieve in him, and few believed in him – few, we are told, even his disciples. Only a few believed and they imperfectly.

Well now, who is Jesus? Christ is the power and the wisdom, but who is Jesus? We have this wonderful thought expressed in Paul's letter to the Philippians (2:6-11): "Though he was in the form of God, he did not consider equality with God a thing to be grasped, but he emptied himself, taking the form of a slave, being born in the likeness of men." That identifies man with a slave, every man. "And being found in human form he humbled himself and became obedient unto death, even death on a cross. Therefore God has highly exalted him and bestowed on him the name" (not an indefinite article) "which is above every name, that at the name of Jesus every knee should bow, in heaven and on earth and under the earth, and every tongue confess that Jesus Christ is Lord, to the glory of God the Father." He gave him the name, and it is above every name, and at that name every power in the world must bend, at the name of names. That is the name called Jesus, which is Jehovah. Jesus simply is Jehovah's name.

The Secret Of Imagination: Imagination Fulfills Itself

Every child born of woman in this world one day wears that name. There is only one name, only one being: Jesus. You go through the same story as told us in the gospel – everyone will – and when he passes through this series of events, that name is conferred. Conferred on the risen Christ. That power is latent in man, that is man's imagination. Where it is lifted up, on that risen Christ, the name Jesus – the divine name, Jesus – is conferred, and that individual then enters a new age. An entirely different age that is immortal, eternal, because until the end of that age we are still subject to being worn out like a garment (as told us in the 51st [chapter] of Isaiah.) So everyone is moving on that wheel that is being worn out, wearing out like a garment and vanishing like smoke, like the heavens. But not one will fail, for God redeems us and God resurrects us, one after the other, lifts us up and confers on that risen Christ the name – the name, Jesus.

When Blake was asked quite innocently about the mysterious name: "What do you think of Jesus?" without batting an eye, Blake replied: "Jesus is the only God," and then hastened to add: "But so am I, and so are you." So in the end, all believed the name where the power – all Christ in man – is lifted up, lifted up so that the whole vast wonderful being that was sunk in man is now awake. What that body is like, I can't describe it to anyone. I can't find words to describe the glory that is yours, for everyone. It certainly isn't this, I assure you, yet I will know you and you will know me in eternity. But for all the sameness of identity we will actually know each other. There will be a radical discontinuity of form (not the form I now wear here today and have for the last fifty-eight years) – but identity – yes, you will know me.

But how to display the glory of the being that you are when you are resurrected? This is shown us by the Sadducees, who do not believe in the resurrection. They are the modern scientists. The Sadducees of 2,000 years ago were the wise men. The Pharisees were the priesthood of the world. The Sadducees were the intellectual giants of that day and they – any more than today – could not even believe in survival, far less resurrection. Like the world today puts the two words together and they speak of survival as resurrection – and they are not. Survival is continuity; resurrection is discontinuity. You leave the field completely and enter the worlds of eternity.

So they ask the question based upon the law of Moses, and Moses said: "If a man's brother dies, leaving a wife but no children, the man must take the wife and raise up children for his brother. Now there were seven brothers; the first took a wife, and died without children; the second and the third took her, and likewise all seven left no children and died. Afterward the woman also died. In the resurrection, therefore, whose wife will the woman be?" (Luke 20:27-33). It is a fable, because they did not believe in the resurrection. "And Jesus said to them, "The sons of this age marry and are given in marriage; but those who are accounted worthy to attain to that age and to the resurrection from the dead neither marry nor are given in marriage, for they cannot die anymore, because they are equal to angels and are sons of God, being sons of the resurrection." They are completely above the organization of sex. What we call sex here, this garment of flesh, are shadows thrown by this fabulous being above. And the body you really have, you are told (as I quoted earlier): "Being in the form of God, did not count equality with God a thing to be grasped, but emptied himself, taking the form of a slave, being born in the likeness of men, didn't think it strange. And being found in human form he humbled himself and became obedient unto death, even death on a cross." And then to find himself with all the limitations of man, all the weaknesses of man, everything that is man? Then God exalted him at the end when he resurrected him and gives him the name. That name is conferred only at resurrection.

So, everyone will get it, for everyone will be resurrected. Then you will not be wearing these bodies, wonderful as they are for us, filled with all the passions of the world, and they are all wonderful – but it is not the body you will wear. You will be completely above the organization of sex. No need for this kind of creativity. Imagination becomes completely awake and you will create at will, and your imaginal act will become an immediate objective fact. And what we call reality today, all this fabulous world of ours – may I tell you I have seen it – it is all imagination. When man has played his part and God has completed his purpose (which is to bring forth from us himself and make us all gods with him) then these garments – made up of all the elements that feel so permanent and so wonderful – they will vanish like smoke. There isn't an element that wasn't brought into being by the creative power of God, by his own wonderful divine imagining, and it is sustained in me because he sustains it by his imaginal act. When he ceases that imaginal act all the elements will melt, all vanish, and the world will be as though it never existed. But you and I will be lifted up above it all into an entirely different world, an eternal world.

So is Christ your imagination? I say Christ is the power and the wisdom of God, and this power and this wisdom creates everything in the world. I can trace to my own being an imaginal act that became fact, then I repeated it and it became fact. If I can repeat it and repeat it, and these imaginal acts externalize themselves in facts, then I have found it. Found that power in myself, for the Bible calls him Christ and personifies it and speaks of [this] presence as a man – but that man is Jesus. Jesus Christ is simply the resurrected being that is God now, because he has resurrected the power within him, which is Christ. Now he is called "the Lord," and everything should bow before him when it happens. I say to you: the day will come you will have the experience, and you will be startled. No one will believe you; they aren't going to believe you anymore than they believed the first person to whom it happened. He is the first that rose from the dead, but no one believed him. Up to the very end who would believe the story?

They were looking for a different kind of Messiah, a conquering hero who would come just like a man out of some glorious background of warriors, and then conquer the enemy of Israel and lead Israel to some victorious end. They always look for that kind of a Messiah. We have them all over the world today, these false Messiah's who promise the nations they will lead them to some victory, even a little temporary victory. That's not Messiah. Messiah hasn't a thing to do with this world; he is resurrected out of this world. This world is vanishing, wearing out just like a garment. Christ in man is the power and the wisdom; and then, that in man that is man's imagination, becomes a mercy because he exercises it lovingly.

If I read John correctly, not only my salvation is dependent on it; I must actually believe in him. Who is the being? My own imagination. If I don't believe and test it – even though I fail – well then, I don't believe in Christ, for Christ is really my imagination, your imagination. So you imagine something lovely of another, and if you don't believe in the reality of that imagination, then you don't believe in Christ. Though you can go to church every day and give ten per cent of your income to the church of your choice – all these things are lovely, give them if you feel that way about it – but that is not Christ. That is not believing in Christ.

To believe in Christ is to see someone in this world, and have a sweet feeling towards that one that hasn't yet realized how to be lovely, something without his knowledge. Then represent him to yourself as though it were true, and believe in the reality of what you have done mentally. Believe in Christ, for all things are possible to Christ. Bring him before your mind's eye and see him as he would like to be seen by himself, as he would like the world to see him. But you do it and believe in the reality of what you have done. That is believing in Christ.

You will be surprised beyond measure how it works. At that very moment, because: "All things by a law Divine in one another's being mingle." At that very moment that you interfere with his life, you reshuffle the entire deck, and all things will completely rearrange to mirror the change that is going to take place in him; and everyone in this world who can aid that change will be used to bring it about without their knowledge or consent. You don't need the consent of any being in the world; if they can be used to externalize what you have imagined, they will be used. And when you least expect it, because you believe in Him, then God resurrects you. Then you will live it out, and you stand bewildered when you see what God did for you.

Everything claimed of him that you thought, that your mother taught you, happened 2000 years ago – it is happening. It didn't stop. Go back and read Paul's letter to Timothy: "Those who teach that the resurrection is past are misleading the faithful." It isn't a past: it took place in one, and it is taking place in unnumbered. It's all over, the crucifixion is over, yes – but not the resurrection. The resurrection is taking place in everyone that is called and lifted up. As we are called, God's mightiest act is performed. and we are lifted up and pass through the series of events leading into the kingdom of heaven. Though we seemingly remain here still wearing this garment for a little while, the garment will be shown you that you will occupy. You can't describe it to anyone, even to your own satisfaction. It is such a living thing, so luminous; it is just light, like the rainbow. You can't describe it to any being in this world who thinks only in terms of a garment of flesh.

Now we are told in the 1st chapter of John (11-13) – he is speaking of an entirely different kind of birth: "And those who believe in his name will be born, not of blood, nor the will of the flesh nor of the will of man, but of God." Not born in any that this (the body) is born. "Flesh and blood cannot inherit the kingdom of God," only Spirit. When you are born, you are self-begotten. You have actually no parents. You come right out of a grain, the mystery of the grain of wheat that falls into the ground. If it doesn't fall into the ground it remains alone; if it falls into the ground, it bears much fruit. The mystery of life through death, for God actually died to become you, to become me.

God is divine imagination and he limits himself to the very limit of contraction, called human imagination, and actually dies in the sense that all the power and all the memory of his glorious being had to be completely forgotten. So the cry on the cross is true: "My God, my God, why hast thou forsaken me." He himself has cried out, because he so completely gave himself to us he suffered total amnesia, complete forgetfulness of his divinity as he became us, and that was divine imagining becoming human imagining. Then we, building our little world – lovely as it is to many of us – it is so different, and the power we exercise is so fragile, compared with that same power when raised up, when lifted up and the great name which is above all names is conferred upon us. And the day will come, without loss of identity you will bear the name "Jesus." Everyone is destined to be Christ Jesus – that power, with the name exercising infinite power – without loss of identity. We will know each other and all glorified, everyone. There is no limitation to the gift. Some will exercise it more than others, but certainly the gift is the same, the gift of Christ Jesus.

So my question, as far as I am personally concerned: "Is Christ your imagination?" I say: yes. And yet don't limit it only to power and wisdom, for the emphasis is not on power and wisdom – it is on redemption, revelation. He reveals himself, and in that very first chapter, the prologue of John. The first eighteen verses are the prologue, and in the very last of the 18th verses he shows you the revelation: "No man has seen God at any time, but the son in the bosom of the father, he has made him known." No one has seen him, but in the bosom of the father there is a son, and he reveals the father.

Then we are told in the 10th chapter of Luke: "No one knows the son except the father. No one knows the father except the son and anyone to whom the son chooses to reveal him." There will come that moment in time when the son reveals you, and you will know your name is Jesus Christ the Lord, for the son is going to call you, "My Lord." He is actually going to call you his father, his Lord, the rock of his salvation, and then you will know who you are.

I can tell you from now to the ends of time, but I can't tell you the condition that experience will carry when it happens. And when it happens to you, it will make no difference to you if all the wise people in the world rise in opposition and tell you: you started from some grand little amoeba. It will make no difference to you whatsoever. This is revelation, and the whole thing is lifted – the veil is lifted – and now you know why you couldn't see the face of the father. You can see him only reflected in the son. There is no mirror to reflect the consciousness of the son. You can't see your face because you are mirrored on earth; but that is not the face, and you only know your face in the beauty of your son. So, everyone in the world is destined to bear the name of Christ Jesus, the Lord.

Now let us go into the silence.

Lecture 5
Neville Goddard
Imagination, My Slave
2-13-1967

I would like to make this series as productive and as helpful as the fall series. For I feel in the fall series that we reached a very high watermark. Not only in what we've accomplished in the world of Caesar but in the spiritual life. Everything here is geared toward a center and that center is God and where are we in relationship to God.

So, we accomplish not only the changes we desire in this outer world, but the real change between the surface mind of ours and the deeper self, which is God. And to accomplish that, I must ask you to do what we did last fall: to share with me your dreams and your visions, and your experiences as you apply this law to accomplish changes in this outer world. That makes it far more real, more wonderful. And if you will share with me, things, we'll all be mutually encouraged by each other's faith.

If you have the faith enough to apply it – when you come up against it, then tell me what happened, so I can then, from the platform tell others. It will encourage those who are present to try it and, therefore, increase their faith. So share with me your dreams. For God is speaking to man through the medium of dreams and when I chose the word God, here, let me make it quite clear. When I use the word Lord, God, Jehovah, Jesus, Christ, I AM, Imagination, to me they are synonymous and interchangeable.

I do not have a God stuck off in space that differs from the one I speak of as I AM. When I speak of Imagination, I speak of God; I speak of Jehovah; I speak of Jesus; I speak of Christ. So, these terms, to me, are synonymous and interchangeable. When I say that Jesus Christ is my deeper self, I could say Imagination is my deeper self and yet my slave for purposes of his own. I personify Imagination for I am a person, and my real being is all Imagination.

The Secret Of Imagination: Imagination Fulfills Itself

Therefore, Imagination, to me, is a person. But this deeper self, and for purposes of his own, he is my slave. So I say he waits upon me, upon you, he waits upon all of us – swiftly, impersonally, without any effort whatsoever. When our will is evil or when it is good; it makes no difference to the deep of myself. I am in a state and I am thinking unlovely thoughts; but he waits upon me just as quickly. And he will conjure for me images of evil out of the nowhere. Let me change the state and feel myself in a state of love, of good, and the same presence will conjure for me, instantly, images of love.

So he waits upon me so quickly; so swiftly. No matter what I am on the surface of this being, he conjures and radiates through me, upon the screen of space, all that I am imagining. So I say the entire outer world is solely produced through imagining. If my outer world is produced solely through imagining, then I cannot change the outer world without changing the imagining.

How long will it take? As long as it takes me to change the state I'm imagining. So I imagine I am this, that, or the other. I don't like what I'm seeing and I hate to admit it's caused by what I'm imagining. If it is caused by imagining, it will take no longer to change it than it takes me to change what I am imagining. Is it true? I ask you to test it. See if it works... if there is evidence for it, does it really matter what the world thinks? If tonight you test it, and it proves itself in performance, will it really matter what anyone in this world thinks about this concept? Not if it proves itself in performance. So I ask you to test it.

Tonight I will share with you one man's experience. One of his many responsibilities in his present job is publishing a magazine. It's very high quality in workmanship and it's brought out in four colors. Before the last issue was to be prepared he became bored and tired with it and did nothing about the content of the magazine. Two weeks before the date of publication, here he was without anything and he had to start from scratch to get the magazine out in two weeks – practically impossible.

The Secret Of Imagination: Imagination Fulfills Itself

Sitting in his office he said, although it didn't mean anything to him, if it came out or not, it means so much to so many people, especially his boss, he was being extremely selfish. Something happened in him and he became completely fired with bringing it out. He said it seemed that stories, art, articles – everything – just came through the walls. He wrote three short pieces himself with so much enthusiasm. He then edited all the articles, stories, all the things to be used and then the men who had never worked on this publication before were assigned to get the whole thing out.

Photographers were taken off their jobs and sent out on assignments and his printers, typographers and everyone else concerned worked three shifts of the two weeks left and they brought it out.

How did it start? Before he started, this is what he did. He knew he couldn't bring out a magazine in four colors in two weeks without any stories, articles, editorial comment, etc., so he created a scene in which he saw his boss holding the issue, with the date sign on it. His boss had an expression on his face that implied complete satisfaction with what he was seeing. Then he heard his boss tell him it was the best issue they had ever published.

During that two-week interval, when his mind would falter, he went back to that one picture of his boss and heard him praise him for the work he had done. He held to the end. The end is where we begin. The end is my beginning. We're always imagining ahead of our efforts. We go to the end – no matter what it is we want – we go to the end. And it calls everything in this world to fulfill itself.

Came the day when the magazine was published. His boss praised him like he'd never praised him before. He said it was the best issue they had ever brought out – just as he had imagined it. And as he had imagined it, it happened in the outer world as fact. When the magazine was out and mailed he went by his boss's office and his boss was happy but skeptical. His boss said he felt they had mailed it out a few days too early – two weeks to bring out a four-color magazine and his boss felt it was mailed a few days too soon!

The above story and the following stories are related. His dry cleaner, whom he likes very much, lost the trousers to his best and most expensive suit. He was beside himself and although the cleaner searched his plant three times, he couldn't find the pants. The cleaner told him to make out a claim but he didn't want money, he wanted his pants.

On the next day, driving to and from his work, he felt the fabric of those trousers on his leg. He also felt it with his imaginary fingers. The next day the dry cleaner called his wife to tell her he had found the pants pinned to a suit that was ready for delivery to another person. So the pants were returned.

So here is the picture and listen to it carefully and apply it to what you will hear this night. It was the Christmas season, and he felt very generous and extravagant; he bought dozens of presents and made out dozens of checks. One day a merchant called his wife to tell her a check she had given him had bounced. She called and told him, and he was beside himself. He knew he had hundreds of dollars more than was necessary in his account. He knew there must have been a mistake. But when he checked his bank statement, which had come a few days before, his face was red and he was humiliated. He had made an enormous error in subtraction and there were no funds.

There was no place for him to turn and the next paycheck was weeks off. Where could he turn to get the money immediately? He wrestled with the problem long after bedtime. He thought of going to his bank the next day, and explain what happened; and then he knew he must have some imaginary image that he could believe. HE MUST HAVE AN IMAGINARY IMAGE HE COULD BELIEVE IN... an imaginal act he could believe in.

He said he could believe in imagining that God was bringing it to pass in the best way for everyone involved; those whom he had unwittingly deceived; those whom he had planned to send presents to and now could not; for everyone involved, everything would be all right.

So he fell asleep in the assumption that God was bringing about the best solution for everyone involved.

The next morning when he got up and started toward the bank, he wasn't altogether sure, so he went back to that assumption that God is bringing about the best solution for everyone. He went to the bank and the cashier sent him to a Vice President who listened to his story and told him he should see the Assistant Manager, who asked him nothing. He just looked him over and asked when he thought he could aright this situation. He told the manager the date of his paycheck and he said, all right, all the checks will be taken care of. He didn't ask him how many checks were yet to be taken care of!

Two days later he received an extra bonus from his boss almost ten times the amount of money due for his checks and one of the reasons was because of the outstanding work he had done on the magazine. And when he received the check he was wearing the suit – lost pants and all!

The next day he went to the bank and made a deposit and he was wearing the suit, and he thought it would be only decent to stop and thank the Assistant Manager for his kindness. He recognized on his face a certain sadness. The Manager said it was because they had not been able to do anything for him as no new checks had come in for them to take care of.

At the end of the letter he said I must tell you imagining creates reality. There is nothing I can do or say to you but "thanks". And it seems so inadequate.

May I tell him, and you, there is nothing you can do for me more than to share with me such experiences. Nothing you can do would please me more. If he had sent me a check, I would have spent it. I have spent everything I have ever earned or what was given me except what my father gave me.

And if that were not the family estate I would have spent it long ago.

But I can't spend experiences. I can only share them. I can tell my friends in New York, in Barbados, in San Francisco. This is like the stories in the Bible. This is taking God's principle and proving it. For his imagination is God. Your imagination is God. Let me repeat it. God, Jehovah, the Lord God, Jesus, Christ, I AM, Imagination, they are all interchangeable.

So I say that imagining is like the creative power in me. "The great creative power of the universe is like imagining in me and underlies all of my faculties, including my perception. But it streams into my surface mind least disguised in the form of productive fancy."

So when he sat there and there was no magazine, no articles – not a thing – and he felt embarrassed and selfish, and that he was letting down all those people who depended on him, he took the end. That's productive fancy. He saw his boss reading the magazine and heard him say it was the best issue yet. He found a scene in which he could believe and all the articles and stories, and art came pouring in. Everything moved forward to the fulfillment of that state.

So, I tell you, imagining does create reality. If you would find God, stop thinking of a little term. You know what he is. He's your own human imagination and he's speaking to you moment after moment through desire. He is speaking in the depths of your soul, through dreams and through visions, and you can tell through your dreams and visions what level you are on relative to God. Everything is relative to God. It isn't relative to anything on the outside world for all that is shadows. It's all relative to God

So where do I stand relative to him? Everything, the most insignificant dream to the outer world, has profound significance to you to whom it is spoken and to God who speaks it to you. And the God in you is your own self. Let me repeat: Jesus Christ is my deeper self and yet my slave. He is the one enslaved in me for purposes of his own and he waits upon me as impartially and as swiftly when my ideas and my thoughts, and my desires are evil as when they are good. He will conjure for me in the twinkling of an eye, ideas of good and evil by the call of my desire. Also, let me wish something and instantly the idea is accomplished. They'll say it came out of your wonderful Imagination. I say that is Jehovah, if you prefer, rather than Jesus Christ. I tell you it is the LORD God. It is your own wonderful human Imagination. That is God. And when you learn to fall in love with it, because he's enslaved himself – poured himself – in you, for you aren't really two, you are an extension of himself being called back level by level by level until finally you are one; you aren't two.

So we are called back from an expulsion. It was a self-expulsion, and we are now called back through these infinite levels of awareness and he reveals to us, through the medium of dreams, the level on which we stand. I take scriptures and find out where I stand by a simple dream. Study scripture.

Paul said, "Learn from us to live by scripture". Is it there? Does it parallel your dream in any way? It doesn't have to be exactly the same thing. He's always talking to you and calling you back to himself through layer after layer until finally you reach home. You and He are one.

So this man had to have something, not only to imagine, but something he could believe. I can imagine anything. You can imagine anything. Is there something you can't imagine? Don't tell me. I can tell you the most fantastic story in the world and you can understand me, but you may not believe me. Therefore it means nothing. So he said he must find something he can imagine that he can believe in. He wanted a scene that would cause no embarrassment to anyone. He could believe in God. He could believe that God is bringing to pass now, in the best possible way for everyone involved, a solution to the situation. He knew God would do it in the best way possible. And so he went about his business the next day in the state that God would do it. He didn't question how, he knew God would do it. And in the end he received a check that was ten times the amount he needed to liquidate all the checks he had passed.

So I say, go to the end. The end is where we begin. You can go on casting shadows and trying to change shadows, and you'll go on forever and ever and you will never change that which is in the shadow. But simply remove the object, which is a state of consciousness, out of the shadow into another desirable light, and remain in it until it casts a shadow.

The shadow will not take long. You are the light of the world. "I AM the light of the world." Do you think another one is speaking? God is speaking. When I say God is speaking I mean your Imagination. Your Imagination is the light of the world. He takes the light to illumine the state and the world outside is only a reflection. It's an act bearing witness to the state in which I have moved. I move into a state. I remain in that state and cast my shadow on the screen of space. When you say, suppose he does this, or that, you are giving all your power, which rightly belongs to you, to the shadow world where it does not belong.

So it's entirely up to you. If you test it tonight it will prove itself in the testing.

So please share with me your letter. Paul asks that those who heard it, those who receive the letter, to share with him, that all of them might be encouraged by each other's faith. So, if man has faith enough to try it, though tomorrow morning is the deadline, based upon Caesar's world, you can try it tonight and move into a different state so that if you have a prospective meeting with someone in the morning, a meeting in which the other person would ordinarily say "if you don't do this or that or else", then in the morning that person may not feel well, or maybe he had to go somewhere else, or maybe he's just forgotten. A thousand and one things could happen to prevent that unpleasant meeting. But everything must happen based upon what you are doing.

You are the causative power. But bear in mind that because you are the causative power, it doesn't work by itself. It works only because you are the operant power.

The next lecture will be Remembrance of Things Future. This is Ecclesiastes one hundred percent, as few in this world will accept it. Remembrance of Things Future: to show you who you really are. I tell you that you are God. I'm not here to flatter you. You and I are one. God is one and here, fragmented on the surface of his dream. And then we are called back to the core. All are called back, and we are one. For we come back one by one by one. The entire outer world is solely produced by imagining. "All that you behold, though it appears without, it is within, in your Imagination, of which this world of mortality is but a shadow."

And if it is a shadow, then let me find that which is causing the shadow. And the cause of the shadow is your imaginal activity. What are we imagining, that is the cause of the shadow that we think so objectively real and is so completely independent of our conception of it. All these things seem so completely independent of our conception of it and they are all cast by our own imaginal activity.

So you get into a state of wealth or health or the state of being wanted, etc; any state, and while you remain in the state, they can do their best to rub out the shadows you are casting but they cannot rub out the cause of it all and it always reproduces itself. The whole vast world is reproducing itself, based upon the state that you occupy.

So they can't rub anything out that you are doing by rubbing out things that you do. No matter what they are doing in the outer world, it is what you are doing within yourself.

Man is all Imagination, and God is man and exists in us and we in him. The eternal body of man is the Imagination and that is God himself, the divine body of Jesus. And we, on the surface, are his master. All are the members of this one divine body and only this one body, all gathered into the unity in the one body, which is God. Call it God or Jehovah, or Jesus Christ or I AM. You can say I AM or Imagination in a group like this that understands and get behind names and surfaces. But in the outer world I wouldn't use it because they wouldn't understand.

And so, if you would use the word Jehovah or Jesus, it jumps up there! But it's not living in space. It doesn't appear in time, away up there thousands of years ago in time. But it jumps if you use the word Jehovah or Jesus. But if you use the word I AM, it can't jump. There's no place you can go. You can't go outside the present moment. And if you actually show people what you mean by it, that I AM is the creative power and you create by imagining, then it's got to be here. You just can't get outside this present moment of time when you use these terms. But you can only use them in a group like this.

I am completely awake and have been sent to tell you what I am now telling you. I'm not talking to another being, I'm only talking to myself; all are wonderful aspects of myself. All. All being withdrawn out of me. All coming back through infinite levels of awareness to the one being that I AM.

What is the most practical in this world is the most profoundly spiritual. Tie them together and reverse them. What is the most profoundly spiritual is the most practical. So he is a practical person, yet the world would call him a dreamer... sitting there doing nothing, a four-color magazine to be done and only two weeks before the deadline. Then everything is thrown in his face and he's working three shifts, and everything is at his disposal – everything is completed and the magazine is mailed "a few days too early".

But just imagine the terrific intensity on his part that he gets a bonus check that is ten times the amount of money he had drawn against his checking account.

So I ask you to continue sharing with me your experiences and your dreams. That is the only way you can say thanks.

(Neville mentions here that in future lectures he will tell the visions of Bob Cruther and his wife and he will explain the depth of meaning in Jan's dream. He says that there is so much more to it than she is aware of.)

Question: A woman, from time to time, works with psychologically disturbed children. To them their world is real. How can she correlate their real world of theirs with the real world she creates for herself and not be one of them?

Answer: No man comes unto me except I call him. And he can only call his own. He can't call another. So here is a disturbance in my world in something that is detached from me, asking for help. I'm going to change my world. I'm going to change that shadow. But it really is reflecting some disturbance in me so I'm going to change it. No matter what the outside world thinks, there are more fashions in the world of medicine than there are in the world of clothes. The most highly flung concept of the imbalanced, or unbalanced, people is simply changeable because it is only a theory. The whole thing is in the eye of the beholder. They come to you for help. Don't try to instantly find out what is causing it. Rearrange the whole thing.

Suppose an individual now sees the world in what we would call a natural way. Persuade yourself that they do and if you can believe it, that person will conform to the image. You don't treat the shadow from the outside; you treat it from the inside.

If the child is born blind, who sinned? No one. Neither the child nor his parents but that the will of God be made manifest. No one did wrong. People cannot understand that. They cannot understand that God is love, infinite love, and he can't hurt another for there is no other – only himself.

So, in this case, it will not only depend on the imaginal act, but on one's ability to believe in the reality of the imaginal act. The potency of the imaginal act is its implication, not the imaginal act. Its potency is its implication. What does it imply? Create a scene implying the child is normal and believe it.

Neville tells the story of the teacher in New York with a problem child who was to be expelled from school. The teacher applied the principal of imagining against almost impossible odds and the situation was completely changed. The child graduated; she was not expelled and all the unpleasantness that was there before, disappeared.

If you take the people in this world, including all the doctors, physicians, vegetarians, those who drink excessively and eat excessively – they all have the same length of time to continue. Few men take care to live well, many to live long. Yet it is within the power of any man to live well; but it is not within the power of any man to live long.

Lecture 6
Neville Goddard
Imagining Creates
6-3-1968

The creator of the world works in the depth of your soul, underlying all of your faculties, including perception and streams into your surface mind least disguised in the form of creative fancy. Watch your thoughts, and you will catch Him in the act of creating, for He is your very Self. Every moment of time you are imagining what you are conscious of, and if you do not forget what you are imagining and it comes to pass, you have found the creative cause of your world.

Because God is pure imagination and the only creator, if you imagine a state and bring it to pass, you have found Him. Remember: God is your consciousness, your I AM; so when you are imagining, God is doing it. If you imagine and forget what you imagine, you may not recognize your harvest when it appears. It may be good, bad, or indifferent, but if you forget how it came into being, you have not found God.

You do not have to be rich to be happy but you must be imaginative. You could have great wealth and be afraid of tomorrow's needs, or have nothing and travel the world over, for all things exist in your own wonderful human imagination.

Let me tell you a story of a lady I know who traveled in her imagination. When this lady was about sixteen she lived in Northern California. She was devoted to her father, who lived high, wide and handsome. He supplied all of the family's needs very well until the day he was killed. Then, overnight, the family discovered they had nothing! Her mother, feeling she could not stand being ridiculed, moved the family to San Francisco, where the girl – although possessing outstanding artistic talent – found employment as a waitress in order to help the family.

Taking the streetcar home from work that first Christmas Eve, she found the car filled with young boys and girls, singing and happy, and she could not restrain the tears.

The Secret Of Imagination: Imagination Fulfills Itself

Lucky for her it was raining, so she extended her face to the heavens and let the rain mingle with her tears. As she tasted the salt of her tears she said to herself: "This is not a streetcar, but a ship and I am not tasting my tears, but the salt of the sea in the wind."

While she physically held the rail of the streetcar, she mentally touched the rail of a ship moving into Samoa. Physically tasting the salt of her tears she imagined it was the salt of the sea. As the streetcar reached its destination, she was entering the bay of Samoa, feeling the moonlight shining on her body and hearing a voice say: "Isn't it a heavenly night."

Two weeks later this girl received a check for $3,000 from a law firm in Chicago. It seems that two years before, her aunt had left the United States, requesting that if she did not return, the money was to be given to her niece.

Within one month, the girl was on a ship sailing for Samoa. Coming into the bay, she saw a ship plowing through the water leaving lovely white foam in its path. As the moonlight touched the wake, its spray touched her face and a man standing near said: "Isn't it a heavenly night." At that moment her outer senses experienced what she had used her inner senses to make real!

Now, imagination – being spiritual sensation – is the creator of the world. With her five senses (sight, sound, scent, taste, and touch) she transformed a streetcar in San Francisco into a ship in the South Pacific, and within one month she physically fulfilled her imaginal act.

Many will say that was just coincidence, but it was not! It is reality, but how do I get you to believe me? But whether you believe me or not, I know from experience that God and you are one grand Imagination, and there is no other God! One day, Imagination in you will awaken and you – fully aware of who you really are – will know that all things are subject to you. That is your destiny.

The Secret Of Imagination: Imagination Fulfills Itself

The present moment is a formed imaginal act. Arrest it, and you can change it in yourself by following the advice given in the 18th chapter of the Book of Jeremiah:

" 'Arise! Go down to the potter's house and I will let you hear my words.' So I went down to the potter's house and there he was working at his wheel. The image in his hand was misshapen, but he reworked it into another image as it seemed good to the potter to do."

The word translated "potter," means imagination, and we are told that the Lord is not only our Father, but the potter, and we are the clay in his hands!

Remember the day your boss criticized you, and you are molding an image of yourself based upon what he said. Being undesirable, that image is misshapen. Unable to discard yourself, go down to the potter's house by taking the same scene and reshaping yourself by remembering the day your boss congratulated you on your accomplishments. Will this act change your world? Yes! I tell you: the God of the universe is shaping you morning, noon, and night, as you accept words, actions, and events from seeming others.

I urge you to shape your world from within and no longer from without. Describe yourself as you would like to be seen by others and believe your words. Walk in the assumption they are true and – because no power can thwart God – what He is imagining, you will experience.

You are not someone apart from God, for I AM cannot be divided. The Lord, our God, is one I AM, not two! If God's I AM and your I AM is the same I AM, define what you would like to be. Then believe you are the Lord! Be like the lady who transformed a streetcar into a cruise. Lose yourself in your new state, while your world on the outside remains, momentarily, the same.

Now, your reasoning mind may say she did have an aunt who had the presence of mind to die and leave her $3,000 at that particular time. And being young she did not consider the future; but I tell you: this is how the law works. It never fails if you will go all out and believe that your human imagination is God.

Because God cannot die, he is a God of the living! So when the garment you now wear comes to its end, you – the being living in it – will continue to live. You will still be in a world just like this one until you awaken from the dream of life. Then you will move into an entirely different age, to realize the oneness of the being that you really are. Until then, believe what I am telling you, for it is true.

When you imagine for a seeming other you are blessed, for there is no other and you are giving your imaginal gift to yourself!

Hear your friend tell you his good news, see the joy on his face, feel the thrill of fulfillment, and let it take place in your world. And as it does, recognize your harvest. Realize you are responsible for its consummation.

The world is yourself pushed out. Ask yourself what you want and then give it to yourself! Do not question how it will come about; just go your way, knowing that the evidence of what you have done must appear, and it will.

Last year, while I was in Barbados, a friend received a call from his mother telling him that his brother had killed a man. As he replaced the phone, a vision appeared in which a woman said: "Find Neville and he will give you the rainbow in the sky." My friend called me in Barbados, and when I heard his story I said: "It is done. God is infinite mercy, and there is nothing but forgiveness of sin."

When the spirit of Christ is formed in you, you will forgive a person, no matter what he has done. Pharaoh would not let his people go because God had hardened his heart, so how can you condemn Pharaoh for something God did? Tonight my friend told me his mother had called to tell him his brother had been set free.

I will tell you now, that no one can reach the end of the journey without having killed someone. Everyone must play every part, so that when memory returns he may forgive all. The part of the thief, the murderer, the rapist and the one raped – every state will be experienced. Anything man can do is recorded in scripture, and to fulfill scripture man must do everything.

Had I not played every part, I would not have been born from above. My friend, who loves his brother and could not understand how he could do such a thing, has murdered, as we all have. We must do everything the world condemns in order for the spirit of Christ – which is continual forgiveness of sin – to be formed within us. And when this happens to you, you will see no one to condemn. It is not that you are indifferent to war or murder, but you will see the world as a play with you – the author – playing all the parts.

Remember: you don't have to abide by anything you dislike. It is but a vessel in your hand which is not properly shaped. Go down to the potter's house and rework it into another vessel as it seems good for you, the potter, to do.

You cannot only rework your concept of self into a new one, but you can rework another. If one is not well or does not earn enough to pay his expenses, the concept is misshapen. You don't ask the vessel if you may rework it, rather you feel as though you have witnessed the change or heard the good news.

There must be action, for an idea alone produces nothing. You must act within yourself by entering the idea. When someone calls or makes a request of you, you must act upon it by producing a motor element within yourself. It may be the sound of their voice telling you it has already happened. Or you may feel the touch of his hand. Whatever you do, it must be something that takes the desire from being an idea and moves it into the creative state of fulfillment.

The very first creative act recorded in scripture is when the spirit of the Lord moved upon the face of the waters. Here is motion. If you would like to be elsewhere, all you need to do is close your senses to the room you now occupy and sense the room where you would like to be. Open your eyes, and your senses will deny any change, for yours was a psychological motion. By closing your eyes the obvious here vanishes, and through the act of assumption, there becomes here. Seeing the world related to your new position, you breathe reality into the state and, having moved from where you are to where you want to be, you have created it.

I know this doesn't make sense, but as Douglas said: "The secret of imagining is the greatest of all problems, to the solution of which every mystic aspires, for supreme power, supreme wisdom, and supreme delight lie in the solution of this far-off mystery."

How is this mystery unraveled? By claiming you are all imagination. Then wrapping yourself in space, and mentally seeing your world relative to your assumed position in space. Do that and you have moved.

President Hoover once said: "Human history, through its many forms of governments, its revolutions, its wars – in fact the rise and fall of nations – could be written in terms of the rise and fall of ideas implanted in the minds of men."

Here you see that the change of governments is the result of the change of ideas implanted in the mind. Can you now see how we are implanting the horrors of the world? Read the morning paper, watch television, or listen to the radio, and you will observe how their words frighten you in order to get your attention. See a headline that someone was murdered and you stop to read it. See another, saying things are fine, and you ignore it, as it would mean nothing. Read the scandal sheet, telling of some prominent person who has been unfaithful and you enjoy a bit of gossip. All of these are ideas implanted in the mind, which cause the rise and fall of nations.

I tell you: imagining creates reality! If you want to change your life you must become aware of the ideas you are planting in the mind of others! When you meet someone who is negative, put a lovely idea in its place. Then, whenever you think of him, imagine he is telling you something lovely. And, because you now walk in a world that is not disturbed by his negative state, when he finds himself no longer thinking negative thoughts, he will never know you were its source. You will know it and that is all that is important.

Become aware of the thoughts you are thinking and you will know a more pleasant life. It makes no difference what others do; plant loving, kind thoughts and you will be blessed in the doing.

Believe me: Here was a child of sixteen who transformed her tears into the salt spray of the sea, a streetcar into a ship, and San Francisco into Samoa. She is blessed, for when it came to pass, she never forgot her moment of despair when she imagined a state and it came to pass.

I ask you now to believe in the invisible God who became you. When you say "I AM", you think of the face you wear, but you are not it. You are so much greater than it could ever be.

One day, God's son David will look into the eyes of the being you really are and call you father. He will not call you by the name of the mask you wear, for David is the express image of your invisibility. Recognizing you as his eternal father, David signifies that your journey into the world of death is at its end. And from that moment on you will share your experiences with anyone who will listen and save everyone you meet.

You will save one who is unemployed by mentally hearing him tell you he is now gainfully employed and making more money than ever before. Having heard his good news, you will subjectively appropriate your objective hope and never turn back by doubting the reality of what you have done. You will simply watch it come to pass. Then you will know that you have found him of whom Moses and the law and the prophets wrote: Jesus of Nazareth, who is the Lord God, and the Father of all!

I have disclosed the one and only source of the phenomena of life. Everything that has ever happened, is happening, or will happen to you, comes from God, who is your own wonderful human imagination. I urge you to use it wisely.

Now a lady wrote me, saying she heard a voice cursing her, and – not understanding – she questioned self and heard the words: "Because I want you."

In the Book of Galatians, Paul tells those who have arrived at the end of their journey, to reject all laws and institutions which would interfere with the direct communication with their individual God.

In the spirit world, all organized societies are personified. Rivers, mountains, cities – everything is human, for God is Man. Even the Los Angeles Woman's Club building is personified in the spirit world. Representing a need of the ladies who own it, when seen in the spirit world, and trying to detach yourself from it, it will curse you, for it wants to feed on you.

So when you leave religious institutions, organizations, customs, and laws that would interfere with your individual direct communion with your God, they will curse you, for they will have lost you. Just leave them alone. I have seen them all and they are nothing more than shadows. Once I saw a monstrous witch in a cave teaching little children the black arts. When she saw me she screamed: "O Man of God, what have you to do with me?"

The Bible tells the same story. Those who teach the black arts and how to hurt people, those who would control your mind and make you dependent upon them, are only personifications of organizations who keep you from contacting the only God who is within you.

Every orthodox religious group would enslave you for the rest of eternity if they could; but when you leave that belief, its personification will curse your leaving, but their curse means nothing. They cannot touch you when you completely reject any intermediary between yourself and God.

The Secret Of Imagination: Imagination Fulfills Itself

Now to come back to tonight's theme: Imagining creates reality! Have you imagined something and it hasn't come to pass? Then what are you imagining right now?

Are you imagining you are John Brown? You were not born knowing you were John Brown. You were born and others began to call you John. As time passed you began to assume you were John Brown and began to respond when you heard the name John.

When you imagined being secure did you forget the feeling? Are you imagining you are secure now? You may have no evidence that you are secure, but as you allow others to tell you how much you are loved and wanted, how successful and famous you are, you will begin to assume it, and imagination will have created its reality. Try it, for that reality you already are!

Now let us go into the silence.

Lecture 7
Neville Goddard
Imagination Fulfills Itself
10-26-1968

I say imagination creates reality, and if this premise is true then imagination fulfills itself in what your life becomes. Although I have changed the words, what I am saying is not new. Scripture says it in this manner: "Whatsoever you desire, believe you have received it and you will." This statement goes back two thousand years, yet even before that Jeremiah tells of the same principle in his story of the potter and his clay.

But until imagination becomes a part of your normal, natural currency of thought, you will not act consciously. Like breathing, this awareness must become so much a part of you that you will not turn to the left or the right to praise or blame anyone. When you know this presence it will not matter if you started life behind the eight-ball, or in a palace; as a poor, or a rich child; you will realize that life is always externalizing what you are imagining.

Lacking the knowledge of this principle, you can reproduce your environment – be it pleasant or unpleasant – forever and ever, as you feed your imagination on what your senses dictate. But knowing this principle, you can ignore the present, and untethered by the so-called facts of life, you can imagine the present as you desire it to be and feed upon your desire, rather than its omission.

Now, imagination cannot be observed as we see objects in space, for imagination is their reality. Faucett gives the name, "God" to the cause of the universe, saying: "God, the creator, is like pure imagining in ourselves. He works in the depths of our soul underlying all of our faculties, including perception, and streams into our surface mind least disguised in the form of productive fancy."

Listen to your thoughts and you will hear God's words! A thought that is not felt produces nothing. But a thought producing motor elements reproduces itself! Catch God in a moment of a motor element such as anger, fear, or frustration, being congratulated or congratulating, and you will know what is going to happen in your world. Unless, of course you arrest your thoughts and revise them. Most of us, however, are not aware of what we are doing, so we do not observe the creator. But we can catch him as he streams into our surface mind least disguised in the form of productive fancy.

If, while riding the bus, driving the car, sitting at home, or standing at a bar, you hear a remark and react by moving on the inside, that remark will fulfill itself in what your life becomes. This principle sets you free, if you are willing to assume its responsibility.

But whether you assume it or not, you will fulfill your every motor element thought anyway. So in the end you will not sympathize or condemn, but simply tell those who may be going through an unpleasant experience of this principle, and – if they accept it – let the principle work in their lives.

Now, the average person in America is either Christian or Jew. Ask any one of them if they believe that imagining creates reality, and the chances are they will give you a negative response. But although they do not know it, if they believe in God they believe in imagination. They may read scripture and accept the words on the surface, but their meaning has not become a part of their thinking.

Last night, for instance, I heard Billy Graham for the first time. Here were thousands of people in the audience listening to a thousand-member choir sing the song, "Oh, how I love Jesus." Now, I don't want to be critical, but when I heard Billy Graham speak I realized that he had not the slightest concept of Jesus, far less his second coming. He said: "If Jesus should come now, just imagine, there would be no more cancer, no more heart failures, and no more death."

Billy Graham believes heaven is made up of flesh and blood bodies in excrementitious states. And they would have to have bathrooms there, if there were no more death. If you were still in a body, that is excrementitious. You would have to take in food which is given you, and what you could not assimilate you would have to expel. And, unless you lost all sense of shame and reverted to the animal world, you would have to have a bathroom. I listened to this man and asked myself: is this the man who was entertained at the White House and received by the Pope at the Vatican? (On the other hand, the Pope is equally silly concerning the mystery of Christ.)

Then at the end of the program, there was an appeal for money. He will give you two books which you hadn't asked for. One interprets the Bible and the other interprets the first one. All you need do is send in your donation to this simple address: Billy Graham, Minneapolis, Minn. "But," said he: "this program is costing us $500,000, and we don't have that sort of money. So if you are alone please send in a contribution. But if you are not alone then take up a collection among all who are with you and send it in." Now, this goes on night after night for one solid week! He is a grand and wonderful being, but he has no concept of the mystery of Christ.

Now, I want to show you what I mean when I say you can be exactly what you want to be. Let me begin by telling you that for the last couple of months I have felt like the devil, yet I knew I was responsible for the hell I found myself in. The doctor gave me every possible test, and when I saw him yesterday he told me I was a dilemma.

Do you know what a dilemma is? It's an argument presenting two or more alternatives equally conclusive against an opponent. In other words, if you start on the assumption that whatever you choose your conclusion will be wrong, you have a dilemma. You can use anything as a dilemma. That's me. My blood indicated one thing in a certain test and the opposite in another. The tests only confirmed what I already knew: that the cause of my discomfort lay in the depth of my soul and not in any secondary cause – such as a thyroid, heart, liver, kidney, or anything outside of myself.

The Secret Of Imagination: Imagination Fulfills Itself

I am wearing a body, but it is not me. I put myself into this body, which limits me. I am its operant power. It cannot be causeful, as it only reflects what I am entertaining in my imagination. I must not justify it, condemn, or excuse myself in any way. Knowing I did not feel well, I changed my feeling, and when the tests (which I had taken to please the one I love) came back, I learned I was a dilemma.

I ask you to take the same responsibility. To not pass the buck to any person, organization, situation, or circumstance, but to discover for yourself that imagining truly does create reality. If the cause of all life is God, then God must be all imagination. And because you can imagine, then – like God – you are pure imagination in yourself. Regardless of what reason and your senses deny, you can imagine anything and bring it to pass if this premise is true.

Now let me share a few wonderful letters I recently received. A lady writes: "In July my car needed repair. As I signed the credit slip agreeing to pay the cost of $62, I imagined it was a check, for I never sign a check unless there is money in the bank to cover it. August and September passed with no request for payment. In September a man stopped by and, eager to sell his house, asked me to list it for him. I told him that I was no longer in the business and recommended my former broker. I forgot all about it, but in October, just before the car repair statement arrived, I received a referral commission from my former broker in the amount of $68. – six dollars more than the cost of the repair of my car.

Here the money – like the story in the 6th chapter of Luke – came to her pressed down, shaken together, and running over. Everyone in the ancient world had a big pocket where grain was placed and pressed down until it ran over. Just like the baker's dozen this lady received her $62 – plus.

Then she said: "For some time now my favorite chair has needed new upholstery. Choosing the material and pattern was easy, but the cost of $87 had to be imagined. So rather than limit myself to an exact figure, I simply imagined my chair as already newly upholstered. While sitting in it, I denied its worn cover, and when thinking of it while in another part of the house, I always saw it as I desired it to be.

In early September, while on vacation, our neighbor had a heart attack. His wife, desiring to be with her husband, asked if their son could stay with us until their return. Since he and our son were playmates and inseparable, John stayed with us for five beautiful weeks, and when his mother asked how much she owed me I kiddingly said, 'Nothing! But, some day when you have an old, worn out hundred dollar bill tucked in your billfold and you don't know what to do with it, you can give it to me.' And the lady replied 'That's exactly what my husband and I agreed to do,' and from her billfold she took a folded hundred dollar bill and gave it to me. That money paid for the chair's new cover, plus an additional $13." Again we see the money came to her pressed down, shaken together, and running over.

When you apply this principle towards the seeming other you are applying it towards yourself, because there is no other. We are told that when Job forgot himself in his love for his friends and prayed for them, his own captivity was lifted. Then all that he seemingly had lost was returned, multiplied one hundredfold.

As you forgive another by thinking of him as you would like him to be and persuading yourself of the reality of your imaginal act, you are forgiving him for what he appears to be by putting him into an entirely different state. Do that and you are substituting a noble concept for an ignoble one. That's forgiveness! Forgiveness tests the individual's ability to enter into and partake of the nature of the opposite. A priest will say: I forgive you, yet when he passes you on the street he remembers what was confessed. If he can remember, he has not forgiven! The memory of what was done or said must be replaced by something else, so that the former can no longer be remembered.

If the present Mrs. Onassis remains Mrs. Kennedy in your eyes you have not forgiven her, because you are still seeing her in the old state. Forgive her by so losing yourself in the idea of her new state that it is all you can remember, and not

The Secret Of Imagination: Imagination Fulfills Itself

the former one. Keep thinking of her in the former state and you have pulled her back into it, for there are only states, externalized.

Now here is another story: My friend went to Pittsburgh this summer to visit a childhood friend, who expressed a desire for a new Baldwin organ. Now, owning an inexpensive organ, my friend told her that every time she sat down to play, to imagine seeing the word, "Baldwin" across the front of the organ and claim it is their top-of-the-line model and paid for. This she promised to do.

Now, the friend's father had departed this world, and when she received a check for $4,500 from his estate, she spent it on necessary home repairs. But when another check in the amount of $3,500 arrived from the estate, she decided to buy her organ. Although the Baldwin top-of-the-line model was priced at $5,000, she was told that it would be going on sale for $4,000, plus they would give her a $1,000 trade-in allowance on her present organ – making the total cost to be $3,000. Contracting for the organ of her dreams, she agreed to pay the $3,000 and the organ was installed.

Although a torrential rain had caused the roof of their home to need replacement, the estimate of $1,700 was delayed; so when it arrived, my friend received a call from her friend asking why the roofer had waited to give his estimate until after the Baldwin had been purchased. Then my friend told her the story of my friend Ann, who lived in New York City.

Ann was a member of the world's oldest profession, that of being a lady of the evening. She often came to my meetings, but this day we met on the corner of Broadway and 72nd Street, where she told me this story. One day, while walking by a hat shop, she fell in love with a beautiful hat in its window with a price tag indicating a cost of $17.50. Wanting it so much, she decided to apply this principle, so in her imagination she placed the hat on her head, and as she walked up Broadway she felt the hat on her head. She would not look in a store window and be disillusioned, and when she arrived home she imagined taking off the hat and placing it on the top shelf before looking in the mirror.

The Secret Of Imagination: Imagination Fulfills Itself

Ten days later a friend called and invited her to lunch. When she arrived, the friend handed her a hat box, saying: "I don't know what possessed me, but I bought this hat and when I brought it home I realized I had made a mistake. I do not like it on me but I think it would look lovely on you, Ann." Opening the box she reached in and brought out – not a hat, but the hat.

Then Ann said to me: "Why didn't God give me the money to buy the hat, instead of giving it to me through a friend?" I asked her if she felt obligated to her friend, and when she shook her head, No, I asked how much she usually paid for a hat. When she told me $4 or $5, I asked if she had ever purchased a $17 hat before. Again the answer was No, and when she admitted to owing two weeks' rent, I said: "If while admiring the hat you found a hundred dollar bill on the sidewalk, would you have bought the hat? I'll answer for you, no you would not. You would have paid your rent and perhaps bought some groceries, but you would not have purchased the hat. Tell me Ann, how much money must God give you to get you to buy a $17 hat? If he gave you a thousand dollars you wouldn't have bought it, for you are not in the habit of buying such expensive hats, so God knows best how to give you the hat you desired."

After telling the story, my friend asked: "How much money must God give you to buy the organ? You have the organ because you imagined it. Now, apply the same principle towards the new roof, for imagination will not fail you. Here is a principle the lady used for her organ, but when a new roof was needed she forgot the source of the phenomena of life. Reason came in and told her all of the money from her father's estate was gone. If you will let it, reason will take this divine gift from you and leave you poor, indeed. For you have the gift of possessing whatever you imagine, if you are faithful to that which you have assumed!

Now, a lady wrote, saying: "I dreamed I was in a large department store with a dear friend who agreed to watch my purse while I shopped. But when I returned, my friend was gone and my purse was sitting in a paper bag on the floor. Upon opening the purse I discovered that $30, and a small card which I carry designating that I am an ordained Unity minister, was missing. I awoke wondering why anyone would want that card."

The card contained the central object of truth in her dream. She has paid the thirty pieces of silver – the price paid for truth – and now she has transcended any ordination in this world. As nice as Unity and all of these groups are, they are playing their parts on certain levels of consciousness. But this lady has gone beyond any man-made ism, be it Unity, Christian Science, or Science of Mind. All of these are man-made doctrines, not based on vision. She was shown that she had paid the price for Christ; and the little card which gave her title to a certain level of consciousness has been removed, for she has transcended the psychological level and entered the third level of the ark of life – the level of vision. She has found Christ because she has paid the price.

May I tell you: you have the power within to create anything! Let people be what they want to be, while you set goals for yourself. It doesn't matter what has happened in your life or what the evidence of your senses tells you, the power of the universe is in you. That power is the Lord Christ Jesus, whose name is I AM. You will never know it however unless you test him, for only then will you realize that Jesus Christ is in you. I was taught Christ was on the outside somewhere in space. But I took the challenge and tested myself, to discover that I AM creative. That I create from within and that my life is the fulfillment of my own imaginal acts. I haven't always been wise in my choice, for imagination is always fulfilling its imaginal state and I have imagined unlovely things and reaped them by becoming the fulfillment of what I was imagining.

Then I became more alert and discovered I could catch Christ as he streamed into my mind least disguised in the form of a creative fancy. If my thoughts were motor driven and they were unpleasant, I knew what to expect unless I revised them. But whether they were pleasant or unpleasant, I knew I would fulfill them.

Envy no one. If a man has $500 million and a girl stands at the top of the social ladder it is because God, in them, had the desire and is fulfilling it. Blake was right when he titled his wonderful picture: "More! More! is the cry of the fool. Less than all is not enough." Scripture tells us: "All thine are mine and mine are thine," for all that God is, is yours, as you inherit God. He is your possession, so whatever God is, when you inherit him less than all is not enough. But the cry of "more" is the cry of the fool, for as long as he wants more he never has enough.

Mrs. Onassis draws from a trust fund of over $20 million. You would think that was enough, but you can adjust yourself to a way of life where it would not be. There are the demands of charities, plus – if you desire to be one of the ten best-dressed in the land, you must have a fortune to gratify that desire. There is nothing wrong with it. I personally have no desire to be named among the externally well dressed. I hope I am internally well dressed. I hope my light is blinding. I hope my garment is so powerful one cannot stand in its presence unless qualified to be there. And if I modify my garment to suit the level upon which another stands, that he may see the being I represent, I do – but certainly not on the outside.

I tell you: imagining creates reality. Believe me, for it is true. Faucett was right when he said," The secret of imagining is the greatest of all problems to the solution of which the mystic aspires, for supreme power, supreme wisdom and supreme delight lie in the far off solution of this mystery.

A friend of mine sent Mr. Faucett my book, and called his attention to the chapter called, "Revision". He also sent a copy to one who was a physicist at one of our great universities. The physicist felt that since the statements recorded there were not scientifically provable, the book was not worthy of his library. While the old gentleman – who was a philosopher and teacher at Oxford University – wrote the sweetest letter, saying: "I do not know who Neville is, but having read the chapter on revision as you requested, I know that he could only have received it from the brothers. No one but the divine society could have dictated this chapter." Here was a man filled with praise for a thought the scientist ridiculed because it was beyond his grasp.

I ask you to take me seriously. Imagination will fulfill itself, so do not limit yourself by anything that is now happening, no matter what it is. Knowing what you want, conceive a scene which would imply you have it. Persuade yourself of its truth and walk blindly on in that assumption. Believe it is real. Believe it is true and it will come to pass. Imagination will not fail you if you dare to assume and persist in your assumption, for imagination will fulfill itself in what your life becomes. Now, you may know of someone who had an assumption but died before it was realized. May I tell you: death does not terminate life. The world does not cease to be at the moment in time when your senses cease to register it. Instead, you are restored to life to continue your journey, and your dreams – unrealized here – will be realized there. You can't stop it, for imagining is forever creating reality.

When my brother, Lawrence, was making his exit from this world, I told my sister-in-law that there was marriage in the next world and she – in a very light vein – said: "I don't want to go now, but do you think Lawrence will be waiting for me so we can get married again?" Well I answered in the same light vein, saying: "God is merciful." I'll let it be at that and you can give any interpretation you want to regarding what I have said. But just imagine two people who have spent their life fighting like cats and dogs – wanting to perpetuate it? No. God is merciful. He really is. Once you have experienced an unhappy state you would have to be a stupid idiot to repeat it. But after the resurrection there is no giving or taking in marriage, for you are above the organization of sex – away beyond it.

Now let us go into the silence.

Lecture 8
Neville Goddard
The Perfect Image
04-11-1969

"He is our peace, who will make us both one by breaking down the wall of hostility, that he may create in himself one new man in place of the two, so bringing peace." This being of peace is a person, not a doctrine or philosophy. He is a person who breaks down the wall of hostility between you who are seated here and your true identity, who is a son of God, one with his Father.

Now, a lady wrote, saying: "I saw myself in vision as radiantly perfect, yet I knew that we were two. Remembering the words 'Be ye perfect,' I knew that at one time I was not, but now my present reflection is one of perfection. Then I awoke, got out of bed and stumbled into the door, then lost my temper and yelled at my children for pouring soap on my nice clean carpet. So it must have happened in some other dimension of my being, for I certainly am not perfect here." She is right. While we wear these garments of flesh and blood, we lose our temper; we run into doors and do all the things people do here. Did not the perfect one, who was the pattern man, call Herod "that fox," and the scribes and Pharisees "Whited sepulchers, outwardly beautiful and inwardly full of hypocrisy and iniquity"? While you are here, encased in your body of flesh and blood, certainly you will lose your temper. Maybe not as you did before you were perfect, but you will to some degree as long as you remain here.

Now, how does he who is our peace, break down the wall of perdition and make the two of us one? By fulfilling his primal wish, which was: "Let us make man in our image, after our likeness." God fell asleep to his true awareness and began a good work in you, which he will bring to completion on the day of Jesus Christ – who is described as being the perfect image of God, one who reflects and radiates God's glory. When his good work is finished, in you, then you – the image – will be superimposed upon him, and you will know yourself to be the Father. There is only God in the world. Having taken upon himself the limitation of man (as you are) he is working you into his image from within. And when you – the made, are as perfect as he – the Maker, you rise as one man, enhanced by reason of the experience of making an image which radiates and reflects your glory. So her vision was perfect, all based upon scripture.

Here is another beautiful one. This lady said, "I found myself in a forest, sitting on the ground leaning against a tree, when I heard a voice calling, 'Father, Father,' but I did not answer, because I did not want to be discovered. Suddenly you appeared, dressed as a shepherd boy, and said to me: 'Why did you not answer me? I have been searching for you.' And I replied: 'You are always searching and finding me, in spite of the fact that the Good Book says I can rest on the Sabbath day.' Then you looked at me and smiled the smile of an indulgent father; yet strangely enough, I – very female – felt I was the father."

In the 4th chapter of Galatians it is said: "When the time had fully come, God sent forth the Spirit of his Son into our hearts, crying: 'Abba! Father!' But the Father, sound asleep in Man, doesn't want to be found, although the Son is always calling: "Rouse thyself, why sleepest thou, O Lord! Awake!" And when one who is called the Son of God awakens to Fatherhood, he is sent into the world to awaken his brothers, but finds they still want to postpone the day of waking, still wanting to hold onto these little garments of flesh and blood. But I will always find you and will not let you rest, for "Truly, truly I say unto you, the dead will hear the voice of the son of God and those who hear it will live." This lady heard the voice and recognized it, so she is not far from waking. Sent as a shepherd boy, the son of God does the Father's will by calling the Father (in Man) to awaken and rise from the dead.

God entered this world for the sole purpose of making you perfect as he is perfect. When his work is finished, he will superimpose himself upon that image and they will be perfectly one. This lady knew she was perfect. She recalled the words: "Be ye perfect." The completed sentence is: "as your Father in heaven is perfect." Yes, be ye perfect for then you become one with your Maker; awake from this dream of life and resurrect from this world of death into a world of eternal life. Without the resurrection you would know infinite circuitry, repeating the same states over and over again. But, after moving around the circle unnumbered times, the perfect image is formed, removing you from the circle to enter a spiral and move up as the person who created it all.

You can join every doctrine, sign every contract between people and nations; yet you will not know perfection until He (in you) finds you perfect and the two of you become one. So, he who is your peace will make you one with him by breaking down the dividing wall of hostility. Then, without telling others you walk knowing who you really are. If you tell the world, they will only laugh at you because – while in this world, like my friend who had the vision – you will run into a door and lose your temper. Everyone is here for a definite purpose, which is revealed through revelations, thereby giving purpose to the whole of life. Without purpose, what does the world have to offer? If you owned everything that you could buy with money, if you had all the money necessary to live comfortably – and your soul is called, what would it matter?

The world may call you dead, cremate your body and scatter your ashes, but you are immortal and cannot die. Rather than being dead, you are in a world just like this one, mentally walking the same tracks over again and again. Oh, maybe you will not experience the same situations, but your world will be just as solidly real. You will return to a lovely twenty-year-old form, to marry, and age, and lose your temper as you bump into a door – until your image is so perfect it is superimposed upon its Maker. Then up you go to know yourself to be the one body, one Spirit, one Lord, one God and Father of all. That is the great living body of the Risen Lord. It seems incredible, but it is true. You are destined to know yourself to be the creator of the world. You are destined to share in the unity of that one body, that one Spirit, that one Lord, that one God and Father of all. I know, for I have experienced it. I was sent back to tell my experiences in the hope that those who are on the verge of moving into the same body, as the same Spirit, may hear my words and be encouraged by them.

Paul makes the statement: "I stand before you on trial for the hope in that promise that God made to our fathers. O King Agrippa, why should it seem incredible to any of you that God raised the dead? Is this not the promise to our fathers?" Search the scriptures and you will find that the promise was made in the 46th chapter of Genesis. "The Lord spoke to Israel in visions of the night saying, 'Jacob, Jacob.'" (As you know, Jacob's name was changed to Israel which means, a man who rules as God because he knows he is God.) Jacob answers: "Here I AM" and the Lord said: "I AM God, the God of your father. Fear not to go down into Egypt, for there I will make of you a great nation. I will go down with you into Egypt and I will also bring you out again." Egypt is not a little place in North Africa; this world of death is Egypt, where everything appears, waxes, wanes, and vanishes. I have gone down into Egypt with you and I will keep my promise and bring you up. When this world was coming to its end, Paul stood in chains before the prince whose kingdom was fading; but he could not let go of it, and said: "Why do you think it incredible that God raises the dead?" and the king could not answer.

I tell you: God literally assumed the weaknesses and limitations of the flesh, in order to know you and to make you into his image. And when that image is perfect as He is perfect, you are no longer two, but one. Then you awake from the dream of life and ascend into your true being, called the kingdom of heaven. Our commonwealth is in heaven and we are sojourners in this strange land where we are enslaved. But have faith and set your hope fully upon that moment in time when the image is perfect. Then it will be unveiled within you to reveal you as the being who made it. Though you are the made, you are the Maker; for the Maker breaks down the wall of hostility between you, making you and He one. Then you return to your heavenly state as the one who came down, but greatly enhanced because of your journey into Egypt.

Having purposely imposed this limitation upon myself, I felt as though I were speaking to another, making requests of him and thanking him for their fulfillment. Now I have no sense of another. I feel only as the one who formed me into his likeness; for when I awoke He and I were not two any more, but one. This lady saw me clothed as a shepherd boy. She saw correctly; for although the Father and the son are one, it is the Spirit of his son who is sent into the heart, crying: "Father, Father." She heard the cry and knew herself to be not only Man, but a father; yet in this world she is very much a lady. She heard my call, yet not wanting to be disturbed she did not respond; but may I tell you, the son of God will never let the Father rest. He is forever calling: "Awake you sleeper! Why sleepest thou, O Lord?" But the Father in you cannot awaken until he has completed his work. He began it in you and will bring it to completion at the day of Jesus Christ.

That day, the image of God himself is formed in you, and you awake to express that image by radiating and reflecting God's glory. Night after night I am crying and crying to the Father in all; and those who hear my voice will begin to awaken from the dream of life and start their journey back to the being they were before that the world was, to find themselves to be more glorious, more wonderful, than they were when they descended.

Tonight some friends are here who haven't heard me speak in a number of years. When they were last with me I was speaking only of the law, as the promise had not fulfilled itself in me. So for their sake let me say: the promise is the law on a higher level, and the law is very simple.

There are infinite number of states. The state of health, the state of sickness, the state of wealth, the state of poverty, the state of being known, the state of being unknown – all are only states and everyone is always in a state. We all have one state in which we are very comfortable, so we return to it moment after moment. That state constitutes our dwelling place. If it is not a pleasant state, we can always get out of it. How this is done is the secret I will now share with you. All states are mental. You cannot remove yourself from your present state by pulling strings on the outside. You must mentally adjust your thoughts to proceed from the desired state, all within yourself. You fell into your present state either deliberately or unwittingly; and because you are its life, the state became alive and grew like a tree, bearing its fruit which you do not like. Its fruit may be that of poverty, or distress, heartache, or pain.

There are all kinds of unlovely fruit. But you can detach yourself from your unlovely harvest by making an adjustment in your human imagination. Ask yourself what you would like to harvest. When you know what it is, ask yourself how you would feel if your desire was ready to harvest right now. When you know the feeling, try to catch it. In my own case I find it easier to catch the feeling by imagining I am with people I know well and they are seeing me as they would if my desire were now a fact. And when the feeling of reality possesses me, I fall asleep in that assumption. At that moment I have entered a state. Now, I must make that state as natural as I have made my present state. I must consciously return to my new state constantly. I must feel its naturalness, like my own bed at night. At first the new state seems unnatural, like wearing a new suit or hat. Although no one knows your suit is new, you are so conscious of it you think everyone is looking at you. You are aware of its fit and its feeling until it becomes comfortable. So it is with your new state. At first you are conscious of its strangeness; but with regular wearing, the new state becomes comfortable, and its naturalness causes you to constantly return to it, thereby making it real.

Now most of us, knowing what we want, construct it in our minds eye, but never occupy it. We never move into the state and remain there. I call this perpetual construction, deferred occupancy. I could dream of owning a lovely home and hope to go there one day; but if I do not occupy it now, in my imagination, I postpone it to another day. I may wish my friend had a better job. I may have imagined him having it; but if I don't occupy that state by believing he is already there, I have merely constructed the state for him but not occupied it. All day long I can wish he or she were different; but if I don't go into the state and view him from it, I don't occupy the state, so he remains in the unlovely state relative to me. This is the world in which we live.

You can't conceive of a thing that is not part of a state, but the life of any state is in the individual who occupies it. Life cannot be given to a state from without, because God's name is "I AM." It is not "You are" or "They are." God's eternal name is I AM! That is the life of the world. If you would make a state alive, you must be in it. If you are in a lovely, gentle, kind state, you are seeing another as lovely, living graciously, and enjoying life to the utmost.

Now, to make that state natural, you must see everyone in your world as lovely, kind, and gentle. Others may not see them in that light, but it doesn't really matter what they think. I am quite sure if I took a survey of what people think of me, no two would agree. Some would say I am a deceiver, while others I am the nearest thing to God. I would find a range stretching from the devil to God, all based upon the state in which the person is in when called upon to define me.

You can be what you want to be if you know and apply this principle, but you are the operant power. It does not operate itself. You may know the law from A to Z, but knowing is not enough. Knowledge must be acted upon. "I AM" is the operant power in you. Put your awareness in the center of your desire. Persist, and your desire will be objectified. Learn to use the law, because there is a long interval between the law and the promise. Those who heard me prior to 1959 are unfamiliar with my experiences since that time, and my words may seem strange to you. I cannot deny the law, for I came not to destroy the law and the prophets, but to fulfill them. This I have done.

I have told you that in the resurrection, Man is above the organization of sex, and that Man can change his sex at will. This week I received a letter telling of a vision which testifies to the truth of this statement. This gentleman is married to a lovely girl and is every bit a man, yet this is his experience. He said, "I found myself lying on a bed feeling as though I am a woman. Desiring a man of oriental descent and olive skin, I assumed I had found him. Instantly he appeared and, although no act was performed, I felt the thrill of imagining and instant fulfillment of my imaginal act. Then I awoke."

This man's vision verifies what I have been telling you: that in the resurrection Man changes his sexual garments at will, and being above the organization of sex, he does not need the divine image of male/female to create. I think his vision is marvelous. When he returned to this world, he was surprised at the experience; but I say to all: you are destined to know you are every being in the world, bar none!

Like the lady who is so feminine, responding when a shepherd boy called her "father". Although she would not answer my call, she knew I would always find her. I always will, for I – the Word of God – was sent as the son of God, and I shall not return to my father void. I must bring back that purpose for which he sent me. I stirred the feeling of the fatherhood of God in her, and I will take back with me those that my father gave me.

But while you are in this world of Caesar, it is important that you master the law. Think of everyone as representing a state. There is no such thing as a good man or a bad man, only good or bad states as you conceive them to be; but the occupant of every state is God. Blake said in his "Vision Of The Last Judgment": "On this it will be seen that I do not consider either the just or the wicked to be in a supreme state, but to everyone of them states of the sleep which the soul may fall into in its deadly dreams of good and evil when it leaves Paradise following the serpent." Identify yourself with a state and you are pronounced by others to be either good or evil; but you are only in a state. Tonight if you are unemployed, or find it difficult to get a promotion in your present employment, remember: the solution to your present state is still a state!

I hope I have made it clear how to move into states. It is done through the act of assumption with feeling and persistence. Assume health. Stand in its center and clothe yourself with its feeling. Persist in claiming a healthy body and a healthy mind, and your assumption will harden into fact as you move into and objectify the state of health.

Now let us go into the silence.

Lecture 9
Neville Goddard
Imagination
7-14-1969

Tonight's subject is Imagination. You read in the 17th chapter of the book of Acts, a story of Paul coming through to the Athenians, and he calls upon these men, for he saw the inscription over and over. He said: "As I passed by...I saw [an altar with] this inscription, 'To an unknown god.' This therefore that you worship as unknown, [this] I proclaim unto you."

"He is not far from each of us, for in him we live and move and have our being."

The great Blake said it differently. This is what Blake said: "All that you behold; though it appears without, it is within, in your Imagination, of which this World of Mortality is but a Shadow." ("Jerusalem")

Then he said: "Babel mocks..." We are all familiar with what Babel represents: the confusion of tongues, no two believing in the same god. Not yet speaking different languages but speaking one tongue, they have different concepts of the creative power of the universe. And so he said:

Babel mocks saying, there is no God, nor Son of God That thou O Human Imagination, O Divine Body art all A delusion, but I know thee O Lord...

He equates God and his son with the human Imagination. To him and to the speaker, Divine Imagination is identical with the word "Jesus." So, when I think of Jesus I do not see a being outside of my own wonderful human Imagination.

Are we not told in Scripture: "With God all things are possible"? We are also told in Scripture: "All things are possible to him who believes." That is Scripture, now. The power of believing is God himself.

So, God in man is man's own wonderful human Imagination.

It's difficult for man to make the adjustment, having been trained to turn on the outside to some god that he worships. We go to church and the mind turns outward to some god, and he paints a word picture of someone before whom we must bend our knee and cross ourselves.

But that's not what Scripture really teaches.

Scripture teaches that the power that creates the entire universe is not without man, but within man, as man's own wonderful human Imagination.

That is the creative power of the world.

All things exist in the human Imagination, so if the word "God" would turn you out, try to make the adjustment within yourself and begin to believe that the God of Christendom, the Lord Jesus of Christendom, is your own Imagination.

If all things are possible to God, and God is your Imagination, then it should be possible for you.

Now, I ask the question. I think I have told it simply enough how you can test it, how you can enter into a state. I think I have told it to the satisfaction of most people that we are the operant power. To hear it, to recite it, commit it to memory, is not enough. We have to apply it, for we are the operant power.

A few days before I closed in Los Angeles, I retired quite early, maybe 9:30 or 10:00 o'clock and I communed with myself. To whom would I turn? "So," I said to myself, "I have said everything that I have heard from within myself, everything that I have experienced concerning the Law, I have told. I have told what I have experienced concerning the Promise. Could I tell them something more about the Law that would make it a little bit more simple? What can I say that I haven't said?"

The Secret Of Imagination: Imagination Fulfills Itself

So, I asked the depth of my own being to show me, to show me exactly what I could say that I haven't said. Well, in the wee hours of the morning, a little after 4:00 o'clock, as I was coming through from the depths of my own being, here is the experience: I am on a spacecraft headed for the moon.

Now, it is all in one's Imagination, for the dreamer is one's Imagination.

That is the cause of all. Now, first of all, let me say that everything in this world contains within itself the capacity for symbolic significance.

So, the moon has within itself the capacity for some symbolic significance. I am headed for the moon.

Now, you have heard the expression time and time again: "Oh, he is reaching for the moon." It could be an ambition based upon your social desire. You want to transcend the limitation of your world where you were born. Or it could be some financial ambition, and friends who know your limitations will say of you: "He is reaching for the moon." Or it could be some tyrant trying to conquer the earth. We have had a Hitler, a Stalin, Alexander the Great, and Napoleon. All these were reaching to conquer the earth, reaching for the moon. Now we are actually on the verge of stepping on the moon, and so we will hit this object in space.

But forget that part of it. I am asking for light so that I can throw some light upon the Law, how to realize my objective in this world in a more simple way than I have so far succeeded in telling it, and this is the vision: I am on this craft and I am headed for the moon. There are others on the craft with me. Instead of landing on the moon, I went into the moon through a very, very large tunnel – a tunnel wider than the depth of this room. The object is dead, dead as dead can be.

I say to someone on the craft: "May I get off?" and he said: "Certainly." I stepped off onto this dead body in space, the moon. There were little objects for sale, objects made on earth and placed on the moon to sell to tourists. They were cheap, cheap beyond measure, made of clay: little cups, little saucers, little plates, little ornaments but the cheapest of cheap! You can't conceive anything cheaper in appearance and in quality.

There they were, made on earth to sell on the moon, just like some sideshow at a carnival. I picked them up, examined them, and thought: "Here, a quarter of a million miles away, man made these things, put them on the moon to sell to tourists." What was the significance of the vision? All of man's ambitions are like clay. They will all turn to dust.

A man died here the other day in Texas. He started out as a poor boy and left an estate of five hundred million dollars, but he left the estate. He had reached the nice, ripe age of seventy-five, but he left every penny behind him. And those who now have billions, they will leave every penny behind them, just as though it is made of dust.

Nevertheless, I asked the question of myself and the depth of my own being answered: so what is the significance of the dream? Tell man, not that he shouldn't have what he wants, certainly he should have it; it is going to be dropped anyway, but he can get it. So, what other point was driven home to me?

This is the point: instead of landing on the moon, I went into the moon.

Blake makes the statement, "If the spectator could enter into the images in his Imagination, approach them on the fiery chariot of his contemplative thought, if he could make a friend and companion of any one of these images in his Imagination" well, he emphasized "enter into the image," not to contemplate it as something on the outside. I contemplate now New York City. I am seeing it from San Francisco. If my desire this night is to be in New York City, I say I can't afford the time, or maybe I can't afford it because of lack of funds, or maybe my commitments will tie me here ?I don't know, yet my desire is to be in New York City.

The Secret Of Imagination: Imagination Fulfills Itself

I must, if I would realize it in spite of the limitations that now surround me (money, lack of time, obligations, call it what you will, I still want to be in New York City. I must enter into the image that is now something on the surface of the mind 'out there,' 3,000 miles away. Standing here, I must shut out the belief that I am in San Francisco.

Knowing New York City quite well, I would assume I am standing in a most familiar part of New York City and let it surround me. I must be in it, and then think of San Francisco. I must now see it 3,000 miles to the west of me, as I now see New York City 3,000 miles to the east of me. If I go into that state and dwell in it and make it natural, though I remain in it only for a little while, a minute or so, then I open my eyes, 'I am shocked' to find that I am still here. I came back here. I have done it. I have entered into the state of my desire and I will move across a bridge of incidents, a series of events that will lead me and compel me to take a journey to New York City.

Now, this I have used only as a spatial example. You can take it in a financial sense, take it in the social world; take it in any way whatsoever. That is what came to me a few days before I closed. For if I could find something more simple to tell them than I think I have told them, this would be it:

To enter into the state and not simply think of the state.

Thinking from it differs from thinking of it. I must learn to think from it.

A man who this night came into a million dollars, from that moment that man is made aware that he has a million, when prior to that he had nothing. He is thinking from the consciousness of having a million dollars. He is not thinking of it; he is walking in the consciousness of having a million dollars. He's not hoping for it, wishing for it; he is actually in it. That is what the vision revealed to me.

Even though at the end of my journey I will leave my things behind me and they will all be as though they were made of clay – all cheaply made, at that, every man, not knowing this

The Secret Of Imagination: Imagination Fulfills Itself

?in fact, how many know it or care to know it? They still want to realize their earthly dreams, and I am all for it; I teach it. But I cannot change the Promise. The Promise is fixed. That is something that will come to every being in this world, for it has been predetermined. But when we are here in this world of Caesar, I can cushion the blows, the inevitable blows, by learning the technique of Law and how to apply it, how to use it.

Now, the thing I quoted earlier, Blake said in this quote from "Jerusalem": "Although I behold Thee not..." Well, here it's perfectly true; I do not observe imagining as I do objects. Imagining is the reality that we name this power called God. So I don't observe imagining; I observe objects, but I don't observe the power in them. That's the greatest secret in the world.

The secret of imagining is the secret of God. Anyone who finds it finds supreme power, supreme wisdom, supreme delight. Everyone should aspire after this secret and try to unravel it, for whatever you find about your own wonderful human Imagination, you are finding about God for your Imagination and God are one and the same. There is no other God. You imagined yourself into this world, and you'll imagine yourself out of it.

You came into the world for a purpose, and when the purpose is fulfilled you will detach yourself from it and return to the being that you were prior to your descent into this world. "Man is all Imagination and God is Man and Exists in us and we in Him. The Eternal Body of Man is the Imagination and that is God Himself." (Blake)

Now, I am not saying it is the easiest thing in the world for you to accept this. It will come to those who have never heard it before as blasphemy. It will come as a shock, an awful shock, when man who is trained to believe in an external God to whom he bows, to whom he prays then to discover that He is not on the outside at all.

As we are told in Scripture: "Do you not know that you are the temple of God, and the Spirit of God dwells in you," and

The Secret Of Imagination: Imagination Fulfills Itself

God is spirit. Well, if God is spirit, and his spirit dwells in you, you can't divide it into different kinds of spirit. God is spirit and his spirit dwells in me. Now, if his spirit dwells in me, I try to find out what that spirit is in me that I can call by another name that is more intimate. Well, I have found it and the spirit of God, which is God himself in me, is my Imagination. And if all things are possible to God and if I can but believe that they are possible to me, well then it's entirely up to me to find out how to believe it.

I imagine, as do you. We cannot imagine differently. All difference lies in content.

So, [my] response to the eternal question: "Who am I?" will determine the circumstances of my life. Who am I? Am I the little one that was born on a tiny little unknown island with no social, intellectual, financial background? Must I accept the limitations of birth? Well most people do. But have I read Scripture? Did I read the words that I AM the temple of the living God, and the spirit of that God dwells in me and all things are possible to that God? Well, I should not allow anything to interfere with my discovery of that spirit in me that is called the "Spirit of God," for if all things are possible to him and he dwells in me, I must make every effort to locate him.

Well, I have located him, and he is my Imagination and I do not differ from any person born of woman. The Imagination in every one is God. But if they have been trained to believe [in] their little beings and my own tiny little Imagination, people will say: "Oh, that's just his imagination."

We are going to the moon. A man imagined it a hundred years ago, Jules Verne. He even imagined the nation that would do it. He said the Yankee know-how, their engineers will contrive the means to get there first. He wrote that 100 years ago, and no matter how others try, we will get there first. We are on the verge of it, but he had to imagine it first.

What is now true was once only imagined. We are in a room. It seems so real. Well, this was once only imagined. You are wearing dresses, you are wearing all kinds of things,

The Secret Of Imagination: Imagination Fulfills Itself

but they had to be imagined first. You go to a tailor or your dressmaker and you pick out the material that you like. It's just a plain piece of cloth. Then you tell your dressmaker or I tell my tailor what kind of a suit I want. So I allow him with his know-how, to take my vision of the kind of a suit that I want. Having picked out the material, he executes it. Now what is then proven when I put it on was first only imagined?

A man imagines a desire, say for wealth. When he becomes wealthy he may forget the means by which it came about and think all the external forces that were used to bring it to pass are the causes. They had to play the part that they played because he imagined what he imagined.

So, I don't differ in the act of imagining from you or any being in the world. The only difference will have to lie in the content of my imagining. What am I imaging? If I imagine something little and feel sorry for myself ?all right, life will prove that I had every reason in the world to feel sorry for myself, because the blows will come to me. And I will turn to the one who gave the blows and blame him or blame them, when the blame (if any) is in myself; for had I not imagined what I have imagined, I could not encounter the conditions that I encountered. This is the Law of Scripture.

We are told: Don't fool yourselves. "Be not deceived. God is not mocked." God is your imagination; he's not mocked. "As a man sows, so shall he reap." (Galatians 6:7) Well, what am I sowing? I AM sowing everything that I AM imagining. That is what I AM sowing, for the only thing I can 'sow' is what I imagine. So, will I now change from an external god to the internal God and find him in myself as my own wonderful human Imagination?

Let Babel rant and say there is no God. Let Babel say there is no Son of God. Then comes that wonderful statement of the prophet, who sees that: "You, O Human Imagination, Divine Body called my Human Imagination, the Body of the Lord Jesus Christ, buried in me."

And were he not buried in me I couldn't even breathe, I couldn't think. But one day he will rise in me and as he rises in me, I AM. I AM he now, but do not know it. When he rises in me I know it then because I rise, not "he" rises. He has become me to the point that we aren't two; we are one.

So, he suffers us.

I say: "I AM in pain." Well, his name is "I AM." That is my Imagination.

I don't say: "My body is weeping," I say: "I AM weeping."

I don't say: "My body is tired," I say: "I AM tired."

So, is not Blake right when he says: "Thou sufferest with me"? Though I do not behold...I can't quite see you as something external. I could not in eternity see myself as something external. I must see it only by reflection and the world undevoutly reflects what I am doing within myself. The day will come I will actually see myself, but not as something external to myself. I will know myself only by reason of the son who stands before me and calls me, "Father."

Then I am looking right into the face of the Son of God, and he will call me "Father." Then, and only then, will I know who I AM.

Everyone will have that experience. One day you will actually see the Son of God, and this relationship is something so deep and so profound there is no uncertainty whatsoever in you when you are confronted. He stands before you, and you see him and you know he is your son and he knows you are his father and there is no uncertainty whatsoever. Only then do you know who you are, that you are God the Father.

Everyone, one day, will have that experience, everyone. I am speaking from experience. I am not theorizing. I am not speculating, but until that day comes let us discover God within ourselves as our own wonderful human Imagination and then test it. "For all things are possible to God; and all things are possible to him that believes." (Mark 9:23)

Well, I can believe but have I made all things come to pass? It can only be my lack of belief if that statement is true. So how then to believe when reason denies it, when my senses deny it?

So reason cannot be the God of whom I speak, for reason will deny it. Doubt cannot be the God of whom I speak for doubt is called in Scripture the devil, 'the demon' and he finds rest only in the human Imagination, the Imagination that will entertain him that's where he went.

If I will have no room in my Imagination for doubt then I am on the road to learning the art of believing. How to believe when reason denies it, when my senses deny it? Well, entering into the image is the most delightful thing in the world. You can try it tonight when we go into the silence. Try it in the simplest little way: putting yourself elsewhere by making 'elsewhere' here, making "there" here and "then" now. And you can do it. It's not difficult if you'll try it.

Let me repeat: we are the operant power. Knowing it is one thing and doing it is another and the minute you try it, you can do it.

Well then, wait. The minute you do it and open your eyes, in the twinkle of an eye you're back here and you will say to yourself, "I didn't do anything; I just did a simple little thing in my Imagination. How on earth could that produce the result when I've just assumed that I've done it?" Well, wait and see if a little bridge of incidents does not quickly appear, compelling you to walk across that bridge of incidents towards the fulfillment of what you have done. It works that way and after you have proven it, the whole world can rise in opposition and it makes no difference to you, you've done it. After you've done it, you keep on doing it and become all the more rooted in who God really is and you'll walk with your head up, walk as you ought to walk as one in whom God dwells.

There's no place in the world more holy than where you are. For wherever you are God is there. There's no church built with human hands comparable to the temple of God and "ye are the Temple of the Living God and the Spirit of God dwells in you." (I Corinthians 3:16) What temple in this world made with human hands could compare to this temple when no hand could make it? It comes into the world and it's a temple of the Living God.

But again, if this is the first time you've heard a thought of this nature, if it's the first time you've been exposed to it, I am not telling you it is not a shock and it's not difficult to accept. It isn't difficult to grasp, but difficult to accept after the training most of us here have had. I know I had it. I was raised in a very wonderful Christian orthodox home, where Sunday school was in order not once a week, but twice a week, grace at the table, Mother reading Scripture to us and interpreting Scripture based upon her concept, which was a secular concept.

To her the Bible was secular history, things that actually happened in her world. She didn't realize that she, as the whole vast world was mistaking personification for persons and the vehicle that conveys the instruction for the instruction itself and the gross perspective for the ultimate sense intended. But Mother was raised that way and she made her exit from this world in that belief.

So, when I was exposed to this at the age of twenty or twenty-two, I must confess I couldn't sleep. It was so completely different that it turned me inside out. I wondered if I'd done the wrong thing to visit this friend. I wondered what on earth have I done? I felt I was a sinful being even to entertain the thought. I had to wrestle with myself and finally, when I put it to the test and it proved itself in performance then I knew that I'd found him.

But you can't find him and not share it with others, as told in Scripture: So Philip found him and he goes and he shares it with Nathaniel. Andrew found him and he goes and shares it with his brother, Peter. Peter didn't find him; his brother found him and then shared it. (See John 1:40-46) So here, we find and we share it. I have found him. All I can do is share him, in the hope that you will accept him.

The Secret Of Imagination: Imagination Fulfills Itself

I know this much: if you believe to the point of acceptance, life will be marvelous for you, perfectly wonderful for this is the one secret in the world that everyone should aspire to solve, for God is that pure imaging in ourselves. He underlies all of our faculties including our perception, but he streams into our surface mind least disguised in the form of productive fantasy. I sit here and have a daydream. Well, that's God in action, but then someone breaks it and I forget it. I didn't occupy it; I simply had a daydream but without occupancy. That's one of the greatest fallacies of the world, 'perpetual construction'. It's a daydream, deferred occupancy. I don't occupy it, I don't go in and possess it and make it mine. If I, in my Imagination, could go right in and possess it and make it mine…If I, in my Imagination, could go right in and possess it and clothe myself with the feeling of the wish fulfilled, actually clothe myself with it by assuming that it's done now, until I feel natural in that assumption and that assumption though at the moment denied by my senses, if persisted in will harden into fact. [a statement made by Anthony Eden at the Guild Hall when he was Prime Minister of England]. So, this is our great secret concerning imagining.

If you doubt it tonight, I would only ask you not to deny it to the point of not trying it, but hold it in abeyance and try it now. Just try it, even if you want to disprove it. I tell you, you will not disprove it. You will in the attempt to disprove it, prove it. And then slowly you will come to completely accept it and then you will walk in the company of God.

You won't have to wait for Sunday morning to meet him in a church or any time of day. No matter where you are, you could be standing in a bar enjoying a drink, having fun at a dance and you are in the company of God. It makes no difference where you are once you know God and God is your own wonderful human Imagination and you'll become extremely discriminating because you'll know you can't entertain these ideas with complete acceptance of them and not reap them in your world.

And who wants to reap the tears forever? So, you become ever more discriminating. Don't think for one second that you'll live a loose life. No. You'll become a far more wonderful person in the world. You hear a piece of gossip, it doesn't interest you.

Today in the morning paper, many people turned right away to the gossip columnist and wondered who is living with whom and they love it. They don't know the people and they will go right out and repeat what this person is paid to print, because it is like almost peeking through the keyhole of someone else's door.

He can't maintain that job. He's paid to be a gossip hound and people read it. Others read only the obituaries to see who's dead. You will not read those pages. You will simply suddenly dwell upon the noble things. Not only for yourself will you do it, your circle will widen. You will. You will think of a friend and if he is distressed, you represent him to yourself as you would like him to be. If he's unemployed, you represent him to yourself as gainfully employed. If he is earning less than what it really takes to live well in this world with his obligations, you represent him to yourself as living well and earning a decent living and assuming full responsibility of his job and you push him in your mind's eye.

So you widen your circle. It's sort of self perpetuating; you take in all because, eventually, "all that you behold, tho it appears Without it is Within, In your Imagination of which this World of Mortality is but a Shadow." (Blake, "Jerusalem")

So, you can't exclude anyone. If you exclude one, it's your own failure. But you don't sit down and work with that one to make it so. You simply assume that it is so. You plant it as lightly as you would if you sowed a field. You don't go out and trample it, you sow the field and it comes up.

Well, this is what I mean by 'Imagination.' I identify my own wonderful human Imagination, when I say ' I,' I AM speaking of all for everyone imagines, so I identify our Imagination with God. That to me is the Lord Jesus. He is buried in us and one day he will rise in us, not as something external to ourselves but he will rise in us as us, after we've gone through the furnaces of experience in this world of Caesar.

Now there's no room for a final death with Christ in man, for Christ resurrects. You say good-bye to a friend who has gone through the gate we call 'death,' but he cannot die. Nothing dies in this world for God is the God of the living. But nothing dies, because the immortal you cannot die and the immortal you is far more real than the garment of flesh and blood that it wears in the world of Caesar.

This is the limit of contraction for a purpose, but when this is burned in the furnace (cremated) you, the occupant, are not burned in the furnace. You are restored, clothed as you are now only the body is young, not a baby, a young body about twenty.

I encounter them all the time and they are young, though when I said good-bye through the gate of 'death,' they were seventy or eighty, my father, eighty-five when he said good-bye, my mother, sixty-one. I met them in their twenties. I am much, much older. I am. I meet them, and they grow. They grow there too; they don't remain twenty. You grow there and you are just as afraid as you are here; and you marry there too and strive there too and die there too, to find yourself restored once more.

And the journey continues until you resurrect. Resurrection is a departure from this age into that age called "the Kingdom of Heaven," but only when he in you resurrects as you, will you leave this world of Caesar. But while you are in it, why not learn his law because the blows are inevitable. Learn the law, that you may cushion the blows.

So, when I know what I want to cushion the problems of the moment, then I will apply it and apply this principle towards anything in my world. And the principle is this: First, you start with desire. Who is desiring? Well, I AM. Well, who is "I AM"? That's God. "That is my name forever and forever," as we are told in the book of Exodus. "Go tell them I AM has sent you. This is my name for all generations, forever and forever." (Exodus 3:15) Therefore, who is feeling? I AM.

Well, that's God! Who is desiring? I AM. Well, that's God and "all things are possible to him." (Mark 9:23).

All right, start right there.

Could I continue desiring if I had it? No I couldn't. If I wanted this room to lecture in when I came here and then I got confirmation from the management that I am allowed to speak in the Marines' Memorial for ten days and the dates are set, could I write him a second letter pleading with him? Could I in any way hope after I had realized it? No, I simply walk in the assumption that I have it. So, when I requested that I have this room for 10 talks, it was granted and from then on I had no more desire for it. The desire was realized.

I had to wait the normal time, the interval of a month, well it was a month ago that I accepted it. Then I came a month later to fulfill it. Well, the same thing is true in all that you do in this world. You simply dare to assume the feeling of the wish fulfilled until it seems natural, until it takes on the tones of reality and when it does, it's done.

And now, trust God. Well, who is God? Your own wonderful human Imagination! Did you imagine it? Well, that's God! Now trust him. Don't turn to any outside power.

The church has just demoted something like a hundred saints, after making fortunes selling little pictures of them. I wonder how many still wear St. Nicholas? They treated him as a saint. It's like treating Santa Claus as a saint. And all these saints – the saint of the road, to protect you against an accident, now they say he never lived. If he never lived why did they ever start it and yet, hundreds of years ago they started this nonsense, so unnumbered millions of these little icons, little medals. Down south our Cardinal admitted that tens of thousands of these little medals, he had put his seal of approval, the Seal of the Cardinal, on the reverse side of that little medal. When they asked him: "Well, now do you regret it?" he said: "No, it was acceptable then and I did it in good faith." But whoever started that nonsense started it for a commercial reason and they made unnumbered millions, hundreds of millions in selling them to the many. And what number of millions of people wore them and are still wearing them – and he never existed! They mount them on the front of their car, on their little trucks, on their bikes and now to discover at this late date...

I've gone out with these friends of mine to greet three fellows who came back from the war. One was a marine; he lost one foot and the arm was completely smashed, one arm. His brother was going into the priesthood and he came back deaf; he was in the army. Another was in the army; he came back with TB. And their mother told me in all innocence and they went along with the mother. "Were it not for St. Christopher they would not have returned." She really believed it, and they believe it and one was three years going for the priesthood when the war broke and he thought it better to serve his country than to become a priest. Then when he came out he gave up completely and got married and has a nice little family. But he believed it and they believed it and the father and the mother believed it.

They entertained me very well, but they knew that I was not safe because I was a Protestant. "Christian" meant nothing to them because you either are a Roman Catholic or you are not a Christian. So, I said to my wife, "What will they think when they find out that I am not a Roman Catholic?" She said, "It doesn't really matter. They love me dearly and I am not one. They know you can't be saved anyway, so what?" So, we all go and have fun. My wife was very, very honest about it for the simple reason her father was that family's closest friend.

And these came back, one with a foot missing, a crushed shoulder. Well, I was in the army too, not as long as these fellows were, but I didn't come back fragmented. I used this principle to get out of the army and I got out honorably discharged. I didn't run away. The very one who said "No" to my request was the very Colonel who called me nine days after I began to apply this principle. I did it quite simply. I made up my mind that I wanted to get out of the army and then I thought, if I were out, where would I be? Well, I wouldn't be here picking up pots and doing all these things in the army and being trained. I would be a civilian in New

The Secret Of Imagination: Imagination Fulfills Itself

York City in my own apartment with my little girl and my wife.

My son was a Marine and he was already in Guadalcanal. He volunteered with my consent for he wasn't more than seventeen when I gave my permission for him to join the Marines.

But having tasted the army life, I wanted no part of it. I was thirty-eight. So, I simply assumed I was a civilian living in New York City with my wife and my little girl, who was only a few months old and the same Colonel who had disapproved my application called me in and said: "Goddard, you still want to get out of the army?" I said: "Yes, sir." And he asked a thousand questions and to each I said: "Yes, sir." Then he said, "All right, bring me in a new application," and that day I was honorably discharged and on a train headed for the fulfillment of my dream.

I simply knew what I wanted; I didn't ask any one's permission. I went to sleep in the barracks with all the boys all around. I didn't tell them what I was doing. As far as they were concerned I was sleeping on that cot. As far as I was concerned I was sleeping in New York City. I went to bed physically on a cot, but in my Imagination in my own bed in New York City. When I thought of Camp Polk, Louisiana it was way down south and I am up here in New York City. And, then the same man who disapproved was the one who actually granted me honorable discharge.

I am speaking from experience; I am not theorizing. I didn't hurt any one. No one was hurt by my application of God's Law. Are we not told: "Whatever you desire, believe that you have received it, and you will?" You will read that in the 11th chapter of the book of Mark: "Whatever you desire...." He didn't say, if it's good for you. He leaves us entirely to make our decision. He actually acquaints us with the law, and leaves us to our decision. So, I was left to my decision. I wanted to get out. The Colonel could tell me nothing to persuade me to change my opinion. If he had said, "No," that was final, I couldn't appeal to some higher echelon.

I could take it only to my commanding officer. Well, he was my commanding officer, and he disapproved it. Well, I came back, I had the paper in my hand, "Disapproved." I went to bed, without his permission, and slept in New York City. I went to bed without anyone in the barracks knowing what I was doing. They saw a man called Neville Goddard sleeping in that bunk but they didn't know I wasn't there, for where could I be save in Imagination? If I am not sleeping here in Imagination, I am not here.

You see the garment that I am wearing, but you would have to find out where I am in Imagination to actually know where I am. You can see the garment, but is the garment the man? I was sleeping in Imagination which is God and "all things are possible to him." Well then, "He" changed the Colonel's decision. He changed his mind. Who is "He"? My Imagination.

God is one. There aren't a million little gods running around. There is only one God. "Hear, O Israel: The Lord our God, the Lord is one." [Deuteronomy 6:4]

Don't look for a second god; there aren't any second gods. And that one God became humanity and in man that one God is man's own wonderful human Imagination: that one God. So it's the 'one' made up of 'others' and that is exactly what the word Elohim means. The word translated 'God' in Scripture is Elohim and Elohim is a compound unity. It's a plural word, one made up of others. We are the 'others' and all collectively make the one Lord, which is called 'I AM.' Well, don't you know that you are, and don't you say: "I AM"? That's God. And can't you imagine? Well, imaging is God in action.

So, what are you imaging? You determine that. For, as I said earlier, I imagine, as do you. We cannot imagine differently. All differences lie in content. What is my response to the eternal question, "Who am I?" That response determines the conditions of my life. Am I a little unknown being, struggling for a dollar to pay rent, to buy food? Well, all right, that's what will happen to me. And there's no being on the outside to change it! I've got to bring about the change within myself. I can borrow money and beg for money and if I remain in that little concept of myself, I will be unable to pay back and will always have to keep looking for someone else to borrow from while I remain in the consciousness of being a little unwanted non-entity.

Let me remain at that moment just what I am and change it now, begin to change my response to the question, "Who am I?" And if God dwells in me I ought to be important, not against someone else in the world. That doesn't make any difference to me what they are. Grant them exactly what they want. If they want riches, let them. What does it matter? If they want to be in the social world at the very top, let them be. No envy whatsoever! If they want to be important in the eyes of the world, let them be important. You have different values. You are in union with God and God is within you and what better companion could you have in this world than to walk in the company of God, walk with him not only on Sunday morning, but every day of the week, knowing who he is?

So, we have to make the decision. "Choose this day whom you will serve." [Joshua 24:15] Will I serve a false god or will I serve the one and only living God? And that one and only living God is your Imagination – my Imagination – and that is the immortal man that cannot die.

Now let us go into the silence.

Good!

When you completely accept this, you will discover you need no intermediary between yourself and God – none! He became you, that you may become God!

Now, are there any questions, please?

Q. [Inaudible]

Neville: I would not say that every dream needs an interpretation. Most of them do, for the universal language, regardless of what tongue you use to express yourself...there is a universal language, and that is the language of symbolism. Unfortunately, we are all past masters at misinterpretation, but there is a language that is a universal language of symbolism. So, I say, everything in this world contains within itself the capacity for symbolic significance.

So, in my vision of the moon I asked for light concerning the law [how] I could tell those that I am trying to teach, a more simple way to realize their objective in this world. And then that night came the vision. It was a very simple presentation, for here the moon is something that man aspires to reach. Long before we entertained the thought seriously of reaching the moon, we used it as an expression, "He is reaching for the moon." And you would say about someone who has no background to even aspire: Why he is crazy! Here is this man without any educational background, and he hopes one day to leave his imprint in the world concerning that which only an educated man can do. Well, they say, "He is reaching for the moon." So, the moon is only a symbol of anyone's desire.

[The same man continued his question.]

Neville: I find myself intuitive enough to interpret the dream of another. I asked down south (I haven't the time here ?it would take more time than I am allotted here for two weeks) but down south they write me letters asking me to explain a dream, which they find difficult to interpret for themselves. And as they grow (and we outgrow in this world) they turn to me for the interpretation of a dream that seems to have no meaning. But every dream has meaning. As we are told in the 12th chapter of the book of Numbers: "God makes himself known unto man in a vision and speaks to him in a dream." (v. 6) Well, if God is my Imagination, and all dreams proceed from my Imagination (that is, my dreams and your dreams) therefore, I must learn the language that it is using to convey to my surface mind this message. So, I cannot discount the simplest dream. It may be produced by some undigested piece of beef, but I don't look upon a dream as the result of any undigested piece of beef. I look upon the dream as my own being – the depth of my being – attempting to reveal something to me in the language of dreams. When it comes to vision, that is something entirely different. This is vision. A vision is just like this, real beyond measure. Question: As regards symbolism, I came across a book that contradicted the whole idea. In other words, this mysticism . . . they say to deny yourself and all images, and leave yourself open and empty to God, and that this is the only way you can have a mystical union.

Neville: First of all, I would not accept that, and I would not say that any person's individual approach is the only way. So, any man who writes a book (and may I tell you, ninety-nine per cent of the books written are a waste of paper) but because a thing is printed, the other person, because he sees it in print, thinks he must be a wise person. "Look, he has a book," but it is sheer nonsense from beginning to end. [The man continued with his question]: It was not just one person; it was several who called themselves, "The Friends of God." I don't know whether you have Neville: Well, for instance, today we have enormous groups of people calling themselves by other names. We just had a huge, big one in New York City where the Yankee Stadium couldn't hold the crowd, and Yankee Stadium can take care of 75,000-odd people in the stands alone. But they were allowed to come down on the grass. Well, if the stands can take care of 70-odd thousand and the field certainly [holds] many, many more ?they estimated they had about 300,000. They called themselves by a very wonderful name in Scripture, and ask any one of the 300,000 who were there to get up and testify from experience about their name. They called themselves "Witnesses." Well, if you are a witness, witness to what? Have you witnessed the birth of God in you? Have you witnessed any of these great mysteries of Scripture?

One of these "Witnesses" came to my door about a year ago (in fact, four of them, but only one came up the stairs). I was busy at the time reading my Bible. I spend hours every day with the Bible. Well, this was about 4:30 or 5:00 o'clock in the afternoon. She came to the door with her Bible all marked up with little pieces of paper, and then, on the street (looking to see what reception she was going to get) there were about three or four down on the sidewalk. She came up and asked me if I would open the door to let her in to explain

God's Word to me. I said: "I am sorry, but you came without an appointment, and I am busy. In fact, I am reading his Word right now." And then something led to something else, and I said: "I am sorry, I am busy, and I have no time to entertain you or to discuss anything with you." Then she started quoting; she wouldn't allow me to brush her off this way, so she started quoting some Scripture. She said, "Do you know what it means?" So, I told her my interpretation of the passage she quoted, and she said to me, "What are you? A Mormon, or something?" So, she was going to have her way, and that's all you can do. So, I said: "I am awfully sorry, my lady, but I cannot give you any more of my time unless it is by appointment. You can't come and ring my doorbell and expect admittance. You can't do it. I have a family, and we live a very quiet and nice life, and we don't have interruptions this way." So, she went on down and they gabbed and pointed their finger up: "Mark that one off; he's going to hell." So, what can you do with people? I mean, leave them alone. You cannot take a man by his nose and put him into a state of consciousness if he resists it. We are told in Scripture, "I will send a famine upon the world; it will not be a hunger for bread or a thirst for water, but for the hearing of the word of God." [Amos 8:11] Well, until that famine is sent upon you by the God within you, the word is not within you. You are more interested in making an extra dollar.

I can't give one person all the questions. I've got to get to someone else.

Q. [Inaudible]

Neville: Ultimately we turn to the One, but we are brothers, as spoken of in Scripture, these words, "He has set bounds to the people, according to the numbers of the sons of God." So, we are brothers; it takes all to make the one. I will never in eternity lose my identity, neither will you, and yet we are one. You are the same God. Of the same son you are the father, as I AM the father. That shows the unity of our being. If you are the father of my son and that one son I know to be my son, and everyone is going to be the father of that son, there is only one Father.

So, Scripture teaches, "There is only one body, one spirit, one hope, one Lord, one faith, one baptism, one God and Father of all" (Ephesians 4:4-6) only one, yet no one is going to lose their identity. I am expanding my identity but there is no loss. When I am embraced by the risen Lord as he wore the "human form divine," which is Love, I answered the question. He asked me to name the greatest thing in the world. When I said, "Love," he embraced me and we fused and became one spirit, one body but I didn't lose my identity. When we separated from that union, I came out as Neville, only within myself I was conscious of a greater self, fully aware of the greater self, without loss of identity. So, everyone here is destined to discover the fatherhood of God as himself through the Son calling him, "Father." Everyone.

Q. [Inaudible]

Neville: My dear, we have eaten of the tree of the knowledge of good and evil. We have enormous pressures in the world to make the world good. We will never bring about an unbalance of good and evil. It is always borne on this tree. This is the tree of the knowledge of good and evil, and it bears equal number of fruit. So, they have all the efforts in the world to make it a better world. They are up the wrong tree. We'll get off this tree of good and evil one day and eat of the tree of life [when] that day comes which comes with the resurrection. And the resurrection is not a collective thing; it is an individual experience. We are called out of this state one by one by one, to unite into a single body, who is the risen Lord. So, everyone is favored.

Ten million dollars for this, a hundred million dollars for that and then just wait a little while, and then at the end of a year a little investigation: a committee is formed to find that those who got the hundred million to dispense it for good, they pocketed it themselves. All of a sudden: "Where is the twenty-seven million dollars in oil gone?" Why, twenty-seven million dollars in oil can't be accounted for.

Somebody had it. They didn't spill it in Santa Barbara. [Ed. note: reference to oil blowout in 1969.] That came out of the sea. So, where are the twenty-seven million? Only that week twenty-seven million dollars worth of oil for our boys in Vietnam and they can't account for it. You see, you find this in every walk of life: good and evil. So don't try to burn it out; you'll not stop the tree from bearing good and evil. You go along your own way in all the lovely things in the world and grant the others to do what they want to do. They are going to do it anyway. When I speak, I want to help every one in this world, individually. I am not for the crowd, to make them all this so-called 'good.' "No one can come unto me, unless my Father call him." (John 14:6) and "I and my Father are one." (John 10:30) Not one could be here tonight if my Father didn't call him. Even those who may never come again were called. This is your first little blow, little explosion.

Q. [Inaudible]

Neville: Why, certainly, you can help anyone in this world, and you will get to the point where you will help everyone. But you are not going to change the nature of the tree. This tree bears good and evil. This is the nature of this world. And all of a sudden you will come out of it and you will eat of the tree of life, and you will see this world so differently, you will be shocked beyond measure.

Q. [Inaudible]

Neville: My dear, the world is dead and people don't know it. Dead, dead as dead can be, even though they are walking it. The day will come that you will have this experience. You will know that what you are feeling within you, you could arrest; and as you look at the people round about you, you arrest their activity within you, and every one stands still. I don't mean they are standing still like soldiers at attention when they can still blink their eyes and move the body; I mean they are dead! They can't move an eye. They are not aware that they are standing still. And if you arrested that motion for 1,000 years, when you released it they would continue on their intention and not know for one moment that they were still for 1,000 years. This is all part of the structure of the universe.

The Secret Of Imagination: Imagination Fulfills Itself

All that is taking place in the world belongs to the eternal structure of the universe. You didn't get created; you are part of the eternal structure. All marriages, all divorces, all love, wayward love, lovely friendships, hates it is all part of the eternal structure of the universe.

So, when we speak of creation, I don't mean erecting a little man of clay. Man was always a part of the structure of the universe. I am not speaking of the creation of life. We are only animated bodies now. The day is coming that we will become life-giving spirits. Then you will see the whole vast world is a dead body, as dead as the moon and all the relationships are worked out in detail. If one could but see with the awakened eye as the child comes through the womb, the whole pattern of its life is there.

Q. [Inaudible]

Neville: Because it's a dead body. It is now animated by the spirit of God, which is called breath, for the word "breath," the word "wind," [and] the word "spirit," are one and the same, both in Greek and in Hebrew. So, it breathes the breath of life into man's body. It is the spirit that possesses the body, that then becomes an animated body – a living being, but not a life-giving spirit. (That [one's] the act of creation.)

[Question concerning assuming the wish fulfilled]...you cannot allow any conscious fears.

Neville: The question is: having assumed the feeling of the wish fulfilled, you cannot deny that in spite of that assumption there are a few conscious doubts and fears. Well, I do not deny that, but practice will make it less and less so and you will trust God so implicitly, not as an external being who may be quite watching you when you are praying. That is what people say, "I wonder if he saw me?" because your Imagination will always...

As we started off the lecture tonight quoting from the 17th chapter of the book of Acts: "You have an unknown god...I will tell you of that unknown God and he is not far off. In him we live and move and have our being." Where could I go, departing from my Imagination? I AM all Imagination and that is God. So whatever I AM imagining, my Imagination is seeing. Eventually you have such complete confidence in Him. Imagination and faith are the stuff out of which man fashions his world. Now, faith is the subjective appropriation of the objective, hope, and faith and Imagination are the stuff out of which we fashion our world.

Good night.

Lecture 10
Neville Goddard
Secret of Imagination
6-21-1971

I thought that this last week should be both practical and idealistic. So we will start on the practical side. He said: "Think not that I AM come to abolish the law and the prophets. I AM come, not to abolish the law and the prophets, but to fulfill them."

Now, the One speaking is now present within you. When He awakes, you will hear these words. You will find them to be your words. That One is your own wonderful human imagination. That One is God!

Imagination is the basis of all that is. What is now proved to be true, as far as we are concerned, was once only imagined. Think of something in the world that is now to you "real" that wasn't first imagined. So, the secret of imagining is the secret of God. And so:

"The secret of imagining is the greatest of all problems, to the solution of which everyone should aspire, because supreme power, supreme wisdom, supreme delight lie in the far-off solution of this mystery."

I can acquaint you with it and then leave you to your choice and its risk, because everything in the world is created by this power. He said:

"I kill and I make alive; I wound and I heal; and none can deliver out of my hand."

"I create the light and make darkness; I create woe and I make weal."

"I, even I, am He, and there is no other God beside me."

That's your own wonderful human imagination. Well, there are secrets to this power, and you and I might experiment. We try to discover the secret. As we discover the secret of imagining, we are discovering the secret of God. So, God and imagination — the human imagination — are synonymous terms. They are interchangeable.

So, when we read that "If we know that He hears us in whatever we ask, we know that we have obtained that which we requested of Him." If we know that He hears us in whatever we ask — no restraint. Now, you may sit down and commune with what you think to be "another" than yourself, God; but because there are billions of us in the world, and there is but one God in this fabulous universe, you might wonder if He heard you. But you have no doubt in your mind if you identify God with your own wonderful human imagination that He heard you!

Can you believe that your own wonderful human imagination is God? So, when you sit down, as told us in the Fourth Psalms "Commune with your own hearts upon your beds, and be silent."

He hears you if you commune with Self, because you believe that communion with Self was communion with God? Can you, now, assume that you are the one that you would like to be? Can you assume that one that you love, is as you would like her — or would like him — to be? Can you really believe that you are answered?

I do not expect tonight that after a certain conception that the child will be born tomorrow.

"The vision has its own appointed hour, it ripens, it will flower; if it be long, then wait, it is sure, it will not be late."

A little child takes nine months, a lamb five months, a chicken 21 days, an elephant — so they tell me — a year or more; a horse, a year anyway. So every conception has its own appointed hour; it ripens, it will flower. If it seems to you long, then wait. It is sure; it will not be late relative to its own nature. So, can I now commune and expect that my communion with Self is communion with God? Can I dare to assume, that I AM exactly what I want to be? Can I dare to assume that I AM where I want to be, even though at the moment my reason denies it, my senses deny it? Will it work? Well, it costs you nothing. Try it! It doesn't cost one penny to try it.

As you are told: "Come, buy wine, buy milk, without money, without price", come and take it. It doesn't cost you one penny to dare to assume that you are where you would like to be, though at the moment reason denies that you are.

Now, I am telling you what I know from experience. When I didn't have a nickel and desired a trip that would cost me well in excess of one thousand dollars, I dared to assume that I was where I would like to be; and I viewed the world from that assumption. Instead of thinking of it, I thought from it. Then I thought of where physically I was, and I saw that place in my imagination two thousand miles to the northwest of me. And I slept in that assumption. And then in a way that I did not consciously devise, — I had no way of knowing how it would ever work; but in a way I did not know, it unfolded; and that assumption hardened into fact.

On the strength of that, I tried it again and again; and when it worked, I began to teach it. I began to tell others that their imagination is the cause of the phenomena of life. This was long before I realized the Promise, as we call it in Scripture. This was only the Law.

So, we are told: "Blessed is the man who delights in the Law of the Lord. In all that he does he prospers."

He didn't say if it was good for you; he left that entirely up to you, to make the decision. You could choose something that may be horrible in time. You choose it without contemplating consequences. But he tells you your imaginal act is a fact.

Now, as He awakens within you, He reinterprets the Law. He can't change the Law. He interprets the Law. Instead of abiding by the external traditions of our fathers, He tells us what the Law really is, when He awakes within us.

The Secret Of Imagination: Imagination Fulfills Itself

"You have heard it said of old, You shall not Commit adultery'; but I say to you, Any man who looks lustfully upon a woman has already committed the act in his heart with her."

He tells us that the restraint of that impulse is not enough. The act was committed at the moment of the imaginal act. I may contemplate the consequences and be afraid — my reputation would be at stake if they catch me. But at that very moment of the imaginal act, that was the fact. That's how he interprets the Law.

Well now, no one can stop you from imagining. No one can stop you from imagining that you are secure; but you may say I have no one in this world to whom I could turn who would leave me a penny, and I have no money. I am beyond the age where they would employ me. And you could give yourself a thousand reasons why it could not be. He is not asking for any reasons. Can you imagine? Well, who can stop you from imagining? That's all that concerns the Awakened Man within you.

Can I dare imagine that I AM what I want to be? Well, I can. I've done it, unnumbered times. I've done it successfully for many that I love dearly and many that I do not know. I have failed often, too; but the failure is in me, it is not in the Law.

Imagination plus faith is the stuff out of which we make the world. We are told all things were made in this manner. "He calls a thing that is not seen as though it were seen, and the unseen becomes seen." And when I come to Him, I must believe that He exists, and that He rewards those who believe in Him. I must have faith in the imaginal act.

If tonight I can stand here and simply quietly imagine a state and really believe that I am in communion with God, when I did that, and that my imaginal act is God's act, — it's not something other than God, — and go unconcerned as to the result, the results will follow me. For that imaginal act was causal at the moment that I did it. The effect when it appears, — I may try to trace the effect to some physical cause and give all credit to a physical cause. I tell you: Every physical effect has an imaginal cause, and not a physical cause. A physical cause only seems; it is a delusion of our fading memory. We do not remember when we imagined it.

In this audience tonight, — and he may not even remember when he did it, — is my dentist. I went to him in great need of a lot of work but I have had dentistry all over this country and in London and Barbados, but it all was horrible. I was always on the move. I was with the theater. Getting in town for a week, what could they do when I needed such work? They patched me up. So when I met him, he gave me a complete job because I was here — living here then.

When one day a tooth gave way which was an anchor tooth, he said to me quite innocently, whether he remembers it or not, "When I saw your mouth and did this, I said to myself, 'This tooth will last thirteen years.'"

It was thirteen years. Had he only said 25, but he didn't think I would live that long! So, thirteen years — out came that anchor tooth, and therefore a complete restructure of my entire mouth. He set it in motion. Whether he remembers or not, he said, "This is going to last thirteen years." He didn't tell me; he didn't have to tell me. That was his imaginal act. I was only the victim of his creative power, Now I am telling you: Don't take anything lightly. You are creating morning, noon and night. Your imaginal acts are God's acts, because your imagination is God! And there is no other God.

"God actually became as we are," — became man, — "that man may become God." And He has set up within Himself — in man — a series of events which He will now unfold within man, which the one in whom He unfolds it, will know, He Is God. He Calls it "giving glory unto man."

"I will not give my glory to another," he said. "I have tried you in the furnace of affliction. For my own sake I do it, for my own sake, for how should my name be profaned? My glory I will not give to another."

God's glory is God, as told us in the 33d Chapter of the Book of Exodus. "I will make my glory to pass before you."

The Secret Of Imagination: Imagination Fulfills Itself

And I will cover you. And when I have passed by, So "my glory" is equated with the "I" of God, for His name is I AM. ' He cannot give His Glory, which is Himself, to another. So, in becoming man, He puts man in the furnaces. But then read the story carefully: "He took upon Himself all of my infirmities and bore my diseases." Who else suffers?

I will say, "But I suffer." Well, that's God. "But I AM feeling it; He isn't." That is no "he"; His name is I AM. So, I feel the pain I feel the infirmity. I feel the diseases. That's God! So, the fool says in his heart:

"There is no God, nor Son of God That Thou, O Human Imagination, art all A delusion; but I know Thee, O Lord, when Thy arisest upon My weary eyes, even in this dungeon, and this iron mill . . . Thou also sufferest with me, although I behold Thee not."

I do not behold imagination as I behold an object in space. I AM the Reality that is named "Imagination"; but I cannot actually see it as an object in space. I see the results of my imagining, but not the Being imagining, for God is invisible.

Then the Voice replied, "Fear not! I AM with you always."

Can I ever get away from imagining? If I fall asleep now and I start dreaming, what is dreaming but imagining? When I awake, He is still with me, and I AM still imagining. " I AM with you always." Only believe in me, that I have power to raise from death Thy Brother who sleeps in Albion."

This comes, now, to the Promise that He made all of us. His Promise is to give Himself to us, as though there were no "others" in the world, — just you, because in giving Himself to you, there is no "other." Your whole vast world is "yourself pushed out." Everything in the world is "yourself pushed out," and you manipulate it by your imaginal acts — everything in the world.

Now, the first act begins with the Resurrection. It's not outside of you, in spite of what you've been taught. The day will come, you will rise within yourself. And that's the only

God that was ever resurrected, Who will ever be resurrected. It's not another; it's you. And when you rise, there is no one on the outside. It's all you. And you are rising in the only tomb in the world where God was ever buried, and that's your own skull. God is buried in the human skull, and that's where He rises. And when He rises, as foretold by His own words in Scripture, he is "born." Resurrection begins the act. That same night, you come out of the tomb, which is your skull, and you are "born from above," — not from the womb of woman where the "garment" was born; you are "born from above," — born of God. "Born not of blood, nor of the will of the flesh, nor of the will of man, but of God." In other words, you are Self-begotten!

God begets Himself, in you, as told us in the Epistle to the Hebrews: He is "bringing many sons to glory", but the sons are numbered. Everyone born of woman is that "son of God," as told us in the 32d Chapter of Deuteronomy: "He has set bounds to the peoples of earth according to the number of the sons of God."

But you will say, "But look, there are three billion in the world." So, what's that? "I will make them more numerous than the stars, more numerous than the sands of the beach", We'll, count them. You can't count the stars. We estimate them to be trillions and trillions. These are the "sons of God," — bringing each that He chooses. He didn't bring all together. He brought a certain number, and that certain number he calls the "second son." The "second son" is represented by this fabulous number. The first son is still waiting to come out. He complains, because the second son went berserk — went amuck and spent his power unwisely, then he came to his senses and returned to his Father, and the Father embraced him and gave him the authority of Himself. He gave him the ring, the robe, the fatted calf — everything for the one who went out and came back to the Father. For His gift is the gift of Himself to you who came out. "I chose you in me before the foundation of the world." That's what we are told.

Let the first son complain. He will complain and complain: "I served you and you gave me nothing," — not even a kid. He said, "My son, all that I have is yours." But the most fabulous gift in the world, or possession in the world, is without meaning unless there is a knowledge of it and a readiness to use it.

Going out as we did, we become aware of our possession; then we can use it. Unless we went out into the world and misused it as we have done, we could not become aware of this power that is our own creative power — our imagination.

I saw it so clearly one night. Here I am in this fabulous field of sunflowers — huge, lovely sunflowers. Each sunflower was a face — the human face, but they were all anchored in the earth. And I walked up and down among the sunflowers. They moved like an orchestra moves; they all moved in unison. If one smiled, they all smiled. If one didn't smile, no one smiled. They simply followed like an orchestra. If one bent over, they all bent over. And everyone did what the whole did. They automatically did it. And I felt, though I was alone — I could walk up and down; they were anchored, — they couldn't do it. I felt that I was freer, limited as I was, than all of them put together, beautiful as they were — these sunflowers were human faces, but they had not gone out.

I was once a part of that infinite garden — not aware of what I possessed; and my Father chose me in Him "before the foundation of the world," and I went out, to go through "hell" in this world, that I may become aware that "All Thine are mine." To become aware that all that is God's belonged to me, I had to go through the furnaces of affliction. And having gone through the furnaces, then He awakes within me; and He tells me how I will know He has awakened within me.

He set up in the beginning the result of the experiences of humanity, and that result is a "son." And the son is called David." And when I find him, I will know he is my son, and I will know the 89th Psalm: "I have found David. He has cried unto me, Thou art my Father, my God, and the Rock of my Salvation." Well, I've found him, and he cried these words to me, and I knew exactly who he was; and I knew then Who I AM. Until then I did not know I was one with God! He is God's Son — God's only Son. Now he's my son!

The Secret Of Imagination: Imagination Fulfills Itself

I tell you, you are going to find him, and he will be your son; and because he is my son, you and I are one. How can he be your son, and I know he's my son, and you and I not be one father? So, we are told, "There is only one body, one spirit, one lord, one God and Father of all." So, in the end, there will not be Greek and Jew, bond and free, male and female; only one — all one in God. And you will be that God! So, this is the Promise that He made.

Now when I read the Bible, I take all the related parts of the Promise and put them all together, for all these things put together will find their fulfillment in you. All His Promises find their "Yes" in Him, as you read it in Second Corinthians: "All the promises of God find their Yes" — their fulfillment — "in Him". So there are 39 books; together they form one Book; but the context, which means the meaning of it, you will find related, scattered over the 39. He pulls from this, from that, from the other, written over the centuries, and pulls it into one pattern, for Christ is the Pattern Man. That pattern is buried in man. It's the only Christ in the world. When the pattern unfolds in man, it unfolds in man as the man in whom it unfolds. And then he knows Who He Is. And he has no doubt in his mind as to who he is. He is the Lord spoken of in Scripture. And that Lord is God the Father. And the whole thing unfolds within him. But he does not abolish the law that he gave; he explains the law as a psychological law and not a physical law.

But if I long after someone at that very moment the act was committed. I state it boldly. I state it boldly, as my dentist stated it boldly. It was committed. So, I went blindly on enjoying everything that he did. It was perfect. And suddenly comes a little bleeding thing which no one could stop. Out comes the tooth. He set it in motion the day he said to himself, — not to me: "It will last thirteen years." I checked it; it was thirteen years.

So Blake said in his wonderful "Jerusalem": "Oh, what have I said? What have I done, Oh, all-powerful human words?" For the word of man is the word of God! "And the word shall not return unto me void, but it must accomplish that which I purpose and prosper in the thing for which I sent it."

But man forgets his word. Then it comes up and he looks for physical causes for it. Now he'll start searching. Do you know what?

Well, "Your system is run down." Did you have fever? Did you have so and so? And you ask a thousand questions of the one: Did you have so and so? You said, No, no, no. No one thinks of that moment when the word went out. Well, the word goes forward, and it cannot return unto us void. It must accomplish that which we purposed and prosper in the thing for which I sent it.

I can see my father now back in 1919. There were ten of us: nine boys and a girl. He was a ship chandler. He had a grocery store, a liquor store and a meat store — a regular little grocery, and he supplied ships; and the ships were bringing the boys back from the first World War, and they would tell him all kinds of stories.

At dinner he would say to my mother, "We will have another war in twenty years. In twenty years there will be another war. It is Germany; but this time, it's going to be Germany and Japan." He didn't mention Italy, but it will be Germany and Japan. "We will again have America as our ally. France will be our ally."

Mother would say, "Joseph, we have nine sons. In twenty years they all will be eligible to go to war." We were all kids in 1919. I was 14 years old.

In 1939, on the 1st day of September war broke — exactly twenty years. What did my father know of any prophecy concerning this? He was only repeating what he had heard from the captains and the stewards and the chief officers as he did business with them. But they were his words! And he said it with conviction, because he believed these men knew what they were talking about.

And our headlines — day after day, they are setting the picture in motion, for tomorrow's confusion. The men are paid enormous salaries to write "scare" headlines. All right, so he writes a scare headline, thinking; It only sells the papers; it isn't going to hurt anyone. But we are going to fulfill them. We fulfill all of our words because God and man are one.

"Man is all imagination; and God is man, and exists in us, and we in Him." "The eternal body of man is the imagination, and that is God Himself."

And God's Word is man's word, and it cannot return unto him void. It just can't if he speaks it with conviction. So, imagination plus faith — these are the very stuff out of which we fashion our world.

So, can I tonight be alone and commune with my Self and be confident that He heard me? I know that I heard myself. Well, that Self is God!

"If we know that He hears us in whatever we ask, we know we have obtained," not are going to, — "we have obtained that which we request of Him." Read it in John's Epistle — the First Epistle, the 5th Chapter, the 15th verse.. We have obtained it! Well, it must take a little interval. It may come tonight, but depending on what seed you planted. One seed will grow overnight; other seeds will take a little longer. But each has "its own appointed hour."

There is not a thing wrong in your noble dreams in this world. You want to be wealthy? What is wrong with it? You want to be anything, — what's wrong with it? Everything is possible.

A friend of mine called me last week. He is now appointed the head purchasing agent for the City of Culver. By law he is not qualified; he does not have the educational background. The law demands you must have a college degree. He doesn't have anything outside of high school. They rearranged it to appoint him the head purchasing agent of Culver City. Why? He came here, he and his brother — I buried the brother a few years ago; he got this job, not dreaming for one moment he could ever transcend it. I said, "Don't for one moment entertain that thought. The job is yours if you want it. Don't push the other one out. Let him go higher. You want to be the Purchasing Agent of the whole City of Culver? You are the Purchasing Agent. Sleep in it just as though it were true, and you hurt no one."

Last week they rearranged the law and he was appointed Purchasing Agent, to take effect in July. Now everything was rearranged. Everything will be rearranged for you.

A friend of mine told me here that you aren't allowed to speak at any state university unless you have a college degree. Well, he confessed that he did not have one, but he was invited by a Professor at U.C.L.A. to take his class — I think there were three or four classes — in the use of imagination, in advertising; so here he went in without the degree, and he was given all the freedom that the Professor enjoyed and he gave either three or four lectures, instead of the Professor who went off for those three or four lectures. So, they suspended the rules. They'll suspend every rule.

They are not supposed to do this, not supposed to do that. Ignore it. Ignore every rule. My friend used to say to me, "You can't smoke in here. Look: 'No smoking.'" And he was a very wonderful lad. He said, "They didn't say it positively." And so he would go right through the gate to the airplane, and I would say, "Mort, you cannot smoke in here. You are not supposed to smoke."

"It didn't say 'positively.'" And here's Mort going right through with his cigarette. No one stopped him. I'm not saying you should do it. He didn't do it to brag. He simply believed in himself. He wouldn't hurt anyone.

Now, you don't have to hurt anyone. I tell you, your own wonderful human imagination is immortal! That's the Man in you that cannot die. I meet them — those who are called "dead," and I tell you, they aren't dead. Nothing dies. Everything is restored. Everything is restored. But the day will come, you will go beyond restoration, and you will resurrect. And who is resurrecting? God. And God-in-you awakens, and you are God, because God is the Father of David. That is the way you know you are God.

"I will tell of the decree of the Lord. He has said unto me, Thou art my son, today I have begotten thee."

These are the words of David, what is going to happen to you. Then you'll know you are God! You have no other way of knowing that you are God unless God's only son calls you "Father," for "No one knows who the Son is except the Father, and no one knows who the Father is, except the Son, and anyone to whom the Son chooses to reveal Him."

So, "No one has seen God; but the only Son, who is in His bosom, has made Him known". He comes out of you, and calls you "Father"! And then you know Who You Are.

And I am telling you, everyone of you — because you and I "were chosen in Him before the foundation of the world" — chosen for the purpose of receiving the gift of God which is His Glory, for He gives me Himself. And in giving me Himself, if He is a father, He gives me His Son. You can't give me yourself in part; give it to me in totality. So, if you are a father, then where is your son? Your son must be my son; and He gives me His Son.

So, "He so loved us He gave His only-begotten Son". To whom? To you, to me, to every child born of woman. So, everyone of us will become fully aware that we are God. And yet, I will know you as Jim; I will know you as Jim, but I will also know that you are God. I will know you as Sol, and know you are God. I will know you as Bill, and know you are God. I will know everyone of you, and the unnumbered billions that are not known to me here, in that day I'll know them all, and still know them all as God, for there's nothing but God!

When the curtain comes down on the final act, we are all God! We are then the Glory of God. So, we will finish the work. He said, "I have finished the work Thou gavest me to do. Now, glorify Thou me with Thine own Self, with the glory that I had with Thee before that the world was." It's returning now. The whole memory returns, and every man becomes God.

But now, do not fail to apply the Law. "Blessed is the man who delights in the Law of the Lord. In all that he does he prospers." You name it, and you can be it. You just name it; and if you dare to assume that you are it and view the world from that assumption instead of thinking of it, you will crystallize it. You will actually manifest it in this world.

That definition of imagination — I'll go along with it to a certain point — up to a point, that things present, are things perceived and called "real"; things absent are called "imagination." But man being all imagination, man must be wherever he is in imagination. So, I need not be anchored to where my senses dictate. I can stand here and assume that I AM elsewhere; and then if I assume that I AM elsewhere, let me anchor myself there and view the world from it. If I view the world from it, I should see this place as I would see it were I were physically there. I can't see it surrounding me and under me, then I did not move in imagination. If I move in imagination, then I must think of where I was physically and see it elsewhere. I can see it where I AM in imagination and be moved, for all motion — well, I can tell myself, If have I moved, by a frame of reference. If I have moved relative to this room, let me look to see, where am I now? I must have moved, for motion can be detected only by a change of position relative to another object. Well here is the object?

I assume that I AM now — and I name it. If I AM elsewhere, let me think of this room. Well, I can't see it as I now see it. If I see it as I now see it, then I didn't move. I can only move if I see it differently.

Well now, if I move and now I am standing in my home, sitting in my chair in the living room, let me think of this club. I must see it away down on Catalina, and feel myself at home on Carol Street, and then think of the club, and it can't be here. It must be way down on Catalina. Then I've moved. For man being all imagination, he must be wherever he is in imagination. If I practice this, it becomes easier and easier.

I just read a story of a very dear friend of mine who used to come to me — not to my meetings, but I would say once a month she came home for a personal appointment in New

York City. She was killed last week in a car driven by her husband. And I can now see this perfectly lovely, gracious lady. She had a home in Oyster Bay, Long Island; and she had her apartment in New York City. Her name is possibly one of the most prominent names in America. The name is Roosevelt. She was of the Teddy Roosevelt branch. Her name was Grace. Her husband was Archibald. Teddy was Governor of New York; he was Vice President of our Country; he was President of our Country — a very powerful, wonderful leader. He did not leave, as so many presidents leave, a fortune. He didn't go in there to make a fortune. He went in there to lead the country. And he said, "I don't consider public opinion. I perform what I think is best for our country. I feed them what they ought to know. I feed them what I think is best for our country."

But he didn't go in there to make a personal fortune, and he came out without a personal fortune. So she — in spite of her name — did not have a personal fortune. She had a home in Oyster Bay, Long Island, and a lovely apartment — beautifully furnished from things that her father-in-law had given her. If she did not rent her New York apartment for the summer, she could not open her home in Long Island. She could not afford it. Being a lovely home in a very wonderful, fashionable area of New York City, she always got a wonderful price paid in advance for the three or four months. Then came the end of a season where they aren't looking for any homes, and she came to see me.

She said, "Neville, I AM desperate. Unless I rent the place in New York City, we can't open our home in Long Island."

I said, "All right. It's rented, and you are living in Long Island ."

"Oh but," she said, "Neville, I can't do that."

I said, "Tonight you sleep in your home in Long Island."

"But," she said, "I can't do that.. How could I go and sleep there?" I said, "You don't do it physically. Tonight you sleep physically in New York City in your apartment; but in your imagination, which is the only reality, you sleep in your home in Long Island, and then you think of your place in New York. The reason why you see it across the East River is because you are physically sleeping in Long Island. And the reason why you are sleeping there is because you rented it. Put them all together; that's why you are there."

She said to me, "If it rents, I'll call you."

I said, "There's no 'if' about it. The only 'if' is if, you do it. Then you'll call me."

I took her to the elevator. She went downstairs, went back to her place. The next day, at 9:00 in the morning, Mrs. Roosevelt is on the phone. She said, "Neville, this is Grace Roosevelt."

I said, "How are you, Mrs. Roosevelt?"

She said, "I AM calling you from Long Island where I slept last night physically. When I went home, no one came at all over the period that you rent places. But as I got home, soon after I got home, an agent called and asked if I could show the apartment. A single man came in. He liked the place. Money meant nothing to him. He said I want immediate possession, but I mean immediate, I mean now!'"

"Well," she said, "I can't get out now. I have to call my husband at the office."

"I don't care what you do. I want immediate possession. And here is my check in advance. Call the bank, to see if the check is good."

She got out that day, She called her husband to meet her, and off they went to their home in Long Island.

Well, she was just killed last week, at the age of 73, I think it was. He was driving; he wasn't injured, and the friend in the car was injured, but Grace was killed instantly. But at least, she learned the Law. She didn't come to the meetings very often because she said in her capacity, she was a pillar of the Episcopal Church in New York City — also in Long Island; it would not be advisable to be seen in my meeting place. That would be "slumming." But she always came to my home with any problem.

One she had with her son. He came back from Egypt where he was in the State Department, and he came with a huge, big beard, and she said, "Neville, I am embarrassed." It was long before people wore beards; today it would be the thing to do, but he came back long before the young fellows wore beards. It was a huge, big beard. She said, "Neville, I am so embarrassed, I just don't want to walk down Fifth Avenue with him. I would make him walk ahead or walk behind me. I don't want to be seen with him. What must I do? Because he gets annoyed and will do nothing that his father or I suggest."

I said, "How would you feel if you kissed him and he had no beard? You would kiss your son, wouldn't you?"

"Oh, yes."

"Well then, put your hand on his face and he doesn't have any beard, and then kiss him and feel that smooth skin that is your son's face when he has no beard."

"All right, I will do that."

She didn't tell me. I opened the morning paper one Monday morning. There was a big fashionable social wedding, and here was Mrs. Roosevelt and her husband, and here is her son and here is the bride coming down the steps of the Episcopal Church, and he has no beard! So the next time she came to see me, I reminded her; I said, "You know, you came here the last time about the beard, and the beard is off."

She said, "Do you know why?"

I said, "Yes, I know why, but you tell me why."

"Well, the girl that he married refused to go through with it unless he shaved." She saw the physical fact.

I said, "No, that wasn't it. You promised me that you would kiss him and feel his smooth skin; and if you would feel the smooth skin, it would come off."

She said, "I did do it, but the girl demanded it."

So, she goes back to a physical causation, and it wasn't so at all. There is no natural effect with a natural cause. Every natural effect has an imaginal cause, and the natural only seems. So she still is going to insist it is because the girl wanted the beard off, and that's why he took it off. Well now, she knows better. She's now in a world just like this. At least she learned the lesson of the Law. She didn't learn the Promise, because when I spoke to her, I did not have the Promise. I had not realized it.

You know the Promise because it only happened to me twelve years ago this coming month. So, those who knew me before, have not heard from me the Promise. Those who have known me since, they know the Promise.

So, I ask you tonight to please take it seriously. Watch your every imaginal act. And I will say to everyone, Don't take anything lightly. Don't voice an opinion that may be embarrassing or hurtful to yourself or to another, even though reason dictates it. Because reason could dictate that this is the fact, for "I've seen so many similar cases that this is going to be so-and-so." Your words are the words of God.

"Oh, what have I said?. What have I done, Oh, all-powerful human words?"

Lecture 11
Neville Goddard
How To Use Your Imagination
1955

The purpose of this record is to show you how to use your imagination to achieve your every desire. Most men are totally unaware of the creative power of imagination and invariably bow before the dictates of "facts" and accepts life on the basis of the world without. But when you discover this creative power within yourself, you will boldly assert the supremacy of imagination and put all things in subjection to it.

When a man speaks of God-in-man, he is totally unaware that this power called God-in-man is man's imagination. THIS is the creative power in man. There is nothing under heaven that is not plastic as potter's clay to the touch of the shaping spirit of imagination.

Once a man said to me, "You know, Neville, I love to listen to you talk about imagination, but as I do so, I invariably touch the chair with my fingers and push my feet into the rug just to keep my sense of the reality and the profundity of things. Well, undoubtedly he is still touching the chair with his fingers and pushing his feet into the rug.

Well, let me tell you of another one who didn't touch with her fingers and didn't push that foot of hers onto the board of the street car. It's the story of a young girl just turned seventeen. It was Christmas Eve, and she is sad of heart, for that year she had lost her father in an accident, and she is returning home to what seemed to be an empty house. She was untrained to do anything, so got herself a job as a waitress.

This night it's quite late, Christmas Eve, it's raining, the car is full of laughing boys and girls home for their Christmas vacation, and she couldn't conceal the tears. Luckily for her, as I said, it was raining, so she stuck her face into the heavens to mingle her tears with rain. And then holding the rail of the street car, this is what she did: she said, "This is not rain, why, this is spray from the ocean; and this is not the salt of tears that I taste, for this is the salt of the sea in the wind; and this is not San Diego, this is a ship, and I am coming into the Bay of Samoa." And there she felt the reality of all that she had imagined. Then came the end of the journey and all are out.

Ten days later this girl received a letter from a firm in Chicago saying that her aunt, several years before when she sailed for Europe, deposited with them three thousand dollars with instructions that if she did not return to America, this money should be paid to her niece. They had just received information of the aunt's death and were now acting upon her instructions. One month later this girl sailed for Samoa. As she came into the bay it was late that night and there was salt of the sea in the wind. It wasn't raining, but there was spray in the air. And she actually felt what she'd felt one month before, only this time she had realized her objective.

Now, this whole record is technique. I want to show you today how to put your wonderful imagination right into the feeling of your wish fulfilled and let it remain there and fall asleep in that state. And I promise you, from my own experience, you will realize the state in which you sleep – if you could actually feel yourself right into the situation of your fulfilled desire and continue therein until you fall asleep. As you feel yourself right into it, remain in it until you give it all the tones of reality, until you give it all the sensory vividness of reality.

As you do it, in that state, quietly fall into sleep. And in a way you will never know – you could never consciously devise the means that would be employed – you will find yourself moving across a series of events leading you towards the objective realization of this state.

Now, here is a practical technique: The first thing you do, you must know exactly what you want in this world. When you know exactly what you want, make as lifelike a representation as possible of what you would see, and what you would touch, and what you would do were you physically present and physically moving in such a state.

For example, suppose I wanted a home, but I had no money – but I still know what I want. I, without taking anything into consideration, I would make as life-like a representation of the home that I would like, with all the things in it that I would want. And then, this night, as I would go to bed, I would in a state, a drowsy, sleepy state, the state that borders upon sleep, I would imagine that I am actually in such a house, that were I to step off the bed, I would step upon the floor of that house, were I to leave this room, I would enter the room that is adjacent to my imagined room in that house. And while I am touching the furniture and feeling it to be solidly real, and while I am moving from one room to the other in my imaginary house, I would go to sound asleep in that state.

And I know that in a way I could not consciously devise, I would realize my house. I have seen it work time and time again. If I wanted promotion in my business I would ask myself, "What additional responsibilities would be mine were I to be given this great promotion? What would I do? What would I say? What would I see? How would I act? And then in my imagination I would begin to see and touch and do and act as I would outwardly see and touch and act were I in that position.

If I now desired the mate of my life, were I now in search of some wonderful girl or some wonderful man, what would I actually find myself doing that would imply that I have found my state? For instance, suppose now I was a lady, one thing I would definitely do, I would wear a wedding ring. I would take my imaginary hands and I would feel the ring that I would imagine to be there. And I would keep on feeling it and feeling it until it seemed to me to be solidly real. I would give it all the sensory vividness I am capable of giving anything. And while I am feeling my imaginary ring – which implies that I AM married – I would sleep.

This story is told us in The Song of Songs, or A Song of Solomon. It is said, "At night on my bed I sought him whom my soul loveth. I found him whom my soul loveth, and I would not let him go until I had brought him into my mother's house, right into the chamber of her that conceived me."

If I would take that beautiful poem and put it into modern English, into practical language, it would be this: "While sitting in my chair I would feel myself right into the situation of my fulfilled desire, and having felt myself into that state I would not let it go. I would keep that mood alive, and in that mood I would sleep." That is taking it "right into my mother's chamber, into the chamber of her that conceived me."

You know, people are totally unaware of this fantastic power of the imagination, but when man begins to discover this power within him, he never plays the part that he formerly played. He doesn't turn back and become just a reflector of life; from here on in he is the affecter of life. The secret of it is to center your imagination in the feeling of the wish fulfilled and remain therein. For in our capacity to live IN the feeling of the wish fulfilled lies our capacity to live the more abundant life.

Most of us are afraid to imagine ourselves as important and noble individuals secure in our contribution to the world just because, at the very moment that we start our assumption, reason and our senses deny the truth of our assumption. We seem to be in the grip of an unconscious urge which makes us cling desperately to the world of familiar things and resist all that threatens to tear us away from our familiar and seemingly safe moorings.

Well, I appeal to you to try it. If you try it, you will discover this great wisdom of the ancients. For they told it to us in their own strange, wonderful, symbolical form. But unfortunately you and I misinterpreted their stories and took it for history, when they intended it as instruction to simply achieve our every objective. You see, imagination puts us inwardly in touch with the world of states.

These states are existent, they are present now, but they are mere possibilities while we think OF them. But they become overpoweringly real when we think FROM them and dwell IN them. You know, there is a wide difference between thinking OF what you want in this world and thinking FROM what you want.

Let me tell you when I first heard of this strange and wonderful power of the imagination. It was in 1933 in New York City. An old friend of mine taught it to me. He turned to the fourteenth of John, and this is what he read: "In my father's house are many mansions. If it were not so, I would have told you. I go to prepare a place for you, and if I go and prepare a place for you, I will come again and receive you unto myself, that where I AM there ye may be also."

He explained to me that this central character of the Gospels was human imagination; that 'mansion' was not a place in some heavenly house, but simply my desire. If I would make a living representation of the state desired and then enter that state and abide in that state, I would realize it.

At the time I wanted to make a trip to the island of Barbados in the West Indies, but I had no money. He explained to me that if I would that night, as I slept in New York City, assume that I was sleeping in my earthly father's house in Barbados and go sound asleep in that state, that I would realize my trip. Well, I took him at his word and tried it.

For one month, night after night as I fell asleep I assumed I was sleeping in my father's home in Barbados. At the end of my month an invitation from my family came inviting me to spend the winter in Barbados. I sailed for Barbados the early part of December of that year.

From then on I knew I had found this saviour in myself. The old man told me that it would never fail. Even after it happened I could hardly believe that it would not have happened anyway. That's how strange this whole thing is. On reflection, it happens so naturally you begin to feel or to tell yourself, "Well, it would have happened anyway," and you quickly recover from this wonderful experience of yours.

It never failed me if I would give the mood, the imagined mood, sensory vividness. I could tell you unnumbered case histories to show you how it works, but in essence it is simple: You simply know what you want. When you know what you want, you are thinking of it. That is not enough.

You must now begin to think FROM it. Well, how could I think from it? I am sitting here, and I desire to be elsewhere. How could I, while sitting here physically, put myself in imagination at a point in space removed from this room and make that real to me? Quite easily. My imagination puts me in touch inwardly with that state. I imagine that I AM actually where I desire to be. How can I tell that I AM there? There is one way to prove that I AM there, for what a man sees when he describes his world is, as he describes it, relative to himself. So what the world looks like depends entirely upon where I stand when I make my observation.

So, if as I describe my world it is related to that point in space I imagine that I AM occupying, then I must be there. I AM not there physically, no, but I AM there in my imagination, and my imagination is my real self!

And where I go in imagination and make it real, there I shall go in the flesh, also. When in that state I fall asleep, it is done. I have never seen it fail. So this is the simple technique upon how to use your imagination to realize your every objective.

Here is a very healthy and productive exercise for the imagination, something that you should do daily: Daily relive the day as you wish you had lived it, revising the scenes to make them conform to your ideals. For instance, suppose today's mail brought disappointing news. Revise the letter. Mentally rewrite it and make it conform to the news you wish you had received. Or, suppose you didn't get the letter you wish you had received. Write yourself the letter and imagine that you received such a letter.

Let me tell you a story that took place in New York not very long ago. In my audience sat this lady who had heard me, oh, numerous times, and I was telling the story of revision –

that man, not knowing the power of imagination, he goes to sleep at the end of his day, tired and exhausted, accepting as final all the events of the day. And I was trying to show that man should, at that moment before he sleeps, he should rewrite the entire day and make it conform to the day he wished he had experienced.

Here is the way a lady wisely used this law of revision: It appears that two years ago she was ordered out of her daughter-in-law's home. For two years there was no correspondence. She had sent her grandson at least two dozen presents in that interval, but not one was ever acknowledged. Having heard the story of revision, this is what she did: As she retired at night, she mentally constructed two letters, one she imagined coming from her grandson, and the other from her daughter-in-law. In these letters they expressed deep affection for her and wondered why she had not called to see them.

This she did for seven consecutive nights, holding in her imaginary hand the letter she imagined she had received and reading these letters over and over until it aroused within her the satisfaction of having heard. Then she slept. On the eighth day she received a letter from her daughter-in-law. On the inside there were two letters, one from her grandson and one from the daughter-in-law. They practically duplicated the imaginary letters that this grandmother had written to herself eight days before.

This art of revision can be used in any department of your life. Take the matter of health. Suppose you were ill. Bring before your mind's eye the image of a friend. Put upon that face an expression which implies that he or she sees in you that which you want the whole world to see.

Just imagine he is saying to you that he has never seen you look better, and you reply, "I have never felt better." Suppose your foot was injured. Then do this: Construct mentally a drama which implies that you are walking – that you are doing all the things that you would do if the foot was normal, and do it over and over and over until it takes on the tones of reality. Whenever you do in your imagination that which you would like to do in the outer world, that you WILL do in the outer world.

The one requisite is to arouse your attention in a way, and to such intensity, that you become wholly absorbed in the revised action. You will experience an expansion and refinement of the senses by this imaginative exercise and, eventually, achieve vision in the inner world. The abundant life promised us is ours to enjoy now, but not until we have the sense of the creator as our imagination can we experience it.

Persistent imagination, centered in the feeling of the wish fulfilled, is the secret of all successful operations. This alone is the means of fulfilling the intention. Every stage of man's progress is made by the conscious, voluntary exercise of the imagination. Then you will understand why all poets have stressed the importance of controlled, vivid imagination.

Listen to this one by the great William Blake:

In your own bosom you bear your heaven and earth, And all you behold, though it appears without, It is within, in your imagination, Of which this world of mortality is but a shadow.

Try it, and you too will prove that your imagination is the creator.

Lecture 12
Neville Goddard
The Secret of Imagining
7-20-1970

Tonight's subject is: "The Secret of Imagining." In almost every particular is the world about us different from what we think it. Why then should we be so incredulous? Life calls on us to believe not less, but more. The secret of imaging is the greatest of all problems, to the solution of which everyone should aspire, for supreme power, supreme wisdom, supreme delight lie in the solution of this mystery.

If you have solved the mystery of imagining you have found Jesus Christ. Jesus Christ is defined for us in scripture as "The power of God and the wisdom of God". As we are told in the eighth chapter of the Book of Proverbs, and Wisdom is speaking now, personified as a little child:

"When He laid out the foundation of the world I was beside Him like a little child I was daily His delight, rejoicing before Him always rejoicing in His inhabited world, delighting in the affairs of men.

He who finds me finds life

He who misses me injures himself; All who hate me love death."

So find that child that is the symbol of Jesus Christ, who is the creative power and the wisdom of God. Believe me when I tell you that this Jesus Christ of scripture is your own wonderful human imagination. "By him all things were made, and without him was not anything made that was made". He is in the world, and the world was made by Him, and the world knows Him not.

Look into the world and name one thing that wasn't first imagined. You name one thing that does not now exist in your imagination just name it. Name anything in the world that does not now exist in your imagination: "All things exist in the human imagination.".

The Secret Of Imagination: Imagination Fulfills Itself

"God is man, and exists in us and we in Him". The eternal abode of man is the imagination; and that is God Himself. Try to disprove it.

God is my pure imagining in myself. He underlies all of my faculties, including perception, but He streams into my surface mind least disguised in the form of productive fancy. I can catch Him in the act of producing these images in my mind. Just try it as you are seated here. Try to think of anything. Try to catch Him in the act of actually producing in your own mind's eye all these images. "For all things exist in the human imagination." But how can I single out one and clothe it so that it becomes an objective fact?

That is the secret, for they all exist within me. But how can I catch one and clothe it? Well I will try to show you tonight what I know from my own personal experience. Scripture teaches it, but it tells it in a strange and wonderful way: how to clothe it.

You see this room in which we are now? It's more real now than your own home is to you; yet you know your home more intimately than you know this room. Yet this room, at the moment, while you are in it, is more real than your own home. How different the cubic reality from the plane of any depiction of it. This room is now so "real" because we are in it, and we are all imagination. We're in it; and to us, it's real. Think of your own home. Do we not have the capacity to draw it, to paint it? But in your mind's eye you have a plane depiction of it, but it's not as real now as the room is. This room is real because we're in it.

Now this is what I mean by making something that is only a thought something that is real. How do I do it? I single out, out of my own wonderful human imagination, that which I want to make real. It's all in you. Then I must enter into it as I have entered into this room. "If the spectator would enter into any one of these images in his imagination, approaching it on the fiery chariot of his own contemplative thought", it would become just as real to him as this room.

You may ask, "What would that do to me? Will it become real in the not-distant future?" I know from my own experience, it will. You can sit here and enter into a state. It may not take on quite the reality of this room, but it will if you persist in it; it will become just like this. When you open your eyes, it vanishes. But does it mean that I tasted that, and that's all? No. Having gone into it, may I tell you, it will follow you? It will not recede into the past as memory; it will advance into the future and you will confront it. This is the secret of imagining, which is finding out the secret of God.

You are an immortal being. You cannot die because you are all imagination. Man is all imagination; and God truly is man; and He exists in us, and we in Him. And that immortal body of man is the human imagination, and that is Jesus Christ Himself, the Eternal Body of man and it cannot die. You cannot die. The body, yes, this will fade; but I AM not the garment that I AM wearing. I AM the wearer of the garment, and the wearer of this garment is all imagination. This is the story that the Bible teaches.

When we read in the Bible: "I, even I, am He. I kill, and I make alive; I wound, and I heal; and there is no god beside me". This is not a being outside of you speaking; this is the Being that you really are, speaking within you, trying to persuade Himself of His own wonderful power to create. It can kill, and yet it can make alive. It can resurrect from the dead. And that is your own wonderful human imagination.

The day will come; you will taste this power that you possess. You will come into a room just like this, and you will still it not by commanding anyone in the room to be still. Leave them just as they are. But you will arrest within yourself an activity that you feel, and as you still it in you, everything that you observe becomes still perfectly still. You could go forward and examine them, and they are dead. Everything is perfectly still and dead. The life is in you. You release the activity, and they once more become animated and continue to do what they intended to do. You could, when you stilled the activity within you, change their motivation; and when you release it, they will do entirely different from what they intended to do prior to your arrestment within you of that activity.

"As the Father has life in Himself, He has granted the Son also to have life in Himself"; and you have that within you. You're not quite aware of it yet, but you will become aware. Those that I am teaching will have dreams, as you have dreams; and in their dreams they will become awake, and then arrest it in the dream and change the motivation and see the intended act change.

Here is one. A friend became aware that she was dreaming, and here's a man who intended to hurt her. He got out of the car and came towards her, and she became afraid; and her fright woke her; but instead of waking on the bed, she awoke in the dream. Then she realized, "This is what he teaches. Now I will simply arrest it." She didn't argue with him; she arrested, within her, the activity that animated him. And she said to him, "You are tired. You need a good hot cup of coffee and then a good sound sleep," and then she told him exactly what he needed, and released the activity within her. He shook his head as though something strange had happened within him, and he got back into the car all in her dream and drove off. You see, she changed his intention towards her.

This may seem impossible to the world. As I started this lecture, almost everything in this world is so completely unlike what it appears to be. And I am telling you from my own experience; I am not speculating. I am not theorizing. The power of which I speak is a power within you. That power is not something on the outside; it's your own wonderful human imagination, and you will learn to control it. Your imagination animates the world in which you live. You change your imagination, and you change the world.

To attempt to change circumstances before I change my own imaginal activity is to struggle against the very nature of my own being, for my own imaginal activity is animating my world. If I believe that I am injured or that others are against me, I have conjured them in my world, and they have to be against me. If I fully believe that all are working towards the fulfillment of my good, they have to work towards the fulfillment of my good. I don't ask them. I don't compel them. I simply do it only within myself, and the whole vast world exists within me. Therefore, it is myself "pushed out." It's objectified. I don't have to change affairs; I only change it within myself; and then everyone, though I know him or not by name, it doesn't really matter, it's myself "pushed out."

I couldn't tell you the atoms of my body, but it is my body. I couldn't tell you if you took the hand off that it's my hand I am looking at, any more than I could tell you your name or anything about you; yet, you are myself "pushed out," as this body is the body I wear. And so, as the body obeys my mind, – you – my "pushed-out" – body will obey my mind too. All I have to do is to concern myself with what I want in this world, and try to keep it within the frame of the Golden Rule; doing unto others only that which I would want done unto me, nothing more than that; hurting no one, doing not a thing to anyone other than that which I would want done unto me.

"You mean, Christ is in me?" Are we not taught that in scripture? "Know ye not that Jesus Christ is in you? Do you not know that Jesus Christ is in you, unless of course you fail to meet the test?". Well then, test it. How would I test it?

A friend of mine, maybe, is unwell; or maybe he's unemployed, or maybe he is not earning enough to meet the obligations of life. All right, he is in me. As I think of him, he's in me. He need not be physically present for me to think of him; he's in me. I think of him; I conjure him. Well, can I change his entire picture in me? I assume that he is talking to me, and he's telling me that he has never had more, he has never felt better; and as I believe in what I am seeing in my own mind's eye, I believe in him. That is Christ in me, and all things are possible to Christ. Well then, test it and see if it works. See if you do not see him in the not-distant future earning more, looking better; and everything in the world that you have done within you, he responds to. He need not praise you or thank you. You don't need his praise; you don't need his thanks. You don't need confirmation from him, other than he does conform to what you have done in yourself concerning him.

You ask no one to thank you. Thank nothing. You are simply exercising the power of God within you. "And the power of God and the wisdom of God is Jesus Christ". And there is nothing in the world but God. It is all God in you "pushed out," and God is your own wonderful human imagination. He can't be closer. God is never so far off as even to be near, for nearness implies separation. He's not separated. God actually, literally became as I am, that I may be as He is. He is not something on the outside. No matter how near He is, He can't even touch me. He actually became me, with all of my weaknesses, all of my limitations; and now I am trying to struggle within myself to find out who I AM, and that's His name. My name is in Him. What's your name? "Go and say I AM has sent you." "Is that you name?" "Yes, forever and forever it is my name." "What name? Jehovah?" "No." "The Lord?" "No, I AM." That's His name. That is His name forever and forever.

Well I cannot say, "I AM," and point elsewhere. I can't say, "I AM," and feel something is near me. It can't even be near. Something can be near to what I AM, but "I AM" can't be near. And that's the name of God forever and forever. So you are the Lord Jesus Christ.

Now a pattern is given to us in scripture by which you will know that you are; and I promise you, from my own personal experience, that you shall have it. It is a true story. The truest story ever told is the story of the Lord Jesus Christ. When He said, "I am the Father," may I tell you, if he's a father, he has a son, hasn't he? Or at least he has a child; but I tell you, it's a son. He said, "When you see me, you see the Father"; but if I look at you and I say, "Well then, you are the father, show me your son." He can't show me His son outside as His son, because He and I are one. He has to show me His son not of blood nor of the will of the flesh; it has to be born, not of blood nor of the will of the flesh nor of the will of man, but of God. And He tells me that He is God, and He tells me that He and I are one. Well then, it can't be born in any normal, natural way. He has to be born of God.

Well then, who is your son? He tells me in scripture that David calls Him, "Father."

"David calls you, 'Father'?"

"Yes." He said, "I inspired the prophets," and read the Prophets; and in the Prophets, David calls the Lord, "my Father."

"You mean, David, then, is my son?"

"Yes, he's my son."

"But I do not know him," you will say.

But I will tell you, from my own personal experience, you will know it because I know it; David called me, "my Father." David called me, "my Lord." David called me the Rock of his salvation. Everything that is said in scripture concerning what he said of the Lord, he said of me. And so, I stood, and here is David, and I knew it beyond all doubt that here is my son, and my son is David, not a David, the David the only David the David of biblical fame. And as he called me, "Father," memory returned.

This is the story of the Christian faith; the fulfillment of all the promises made in the Old Testament. The Old Testament is only a prophetic blueprint of the life of Jesus Christ. It's an adumbration, a foreshadowing in a not-altogether conclusive or immediately evident way; but as it unfolds within you, it's nothing more than God's memory returning. But having become you, it becomes your memory returning, and you awaken as God Himself. And there is nothing in the world like God.

Now you ask, what, all the horrors of the world, the pain, the suffering? Yes. It takes all the "furnaces" to prepare you to receive the gift that He gives, and the gift is Himself. God actually became you. He gave Himself to you, that you may be God. And God in you is your own wonderful human imagination, that's God.

Now tonight try it. I ask you to believe me. But whether you believe me or not, try it anyway. Take a friend of yours and bring him before your mind's eye, and then talk to him from the premise of your desire for him fulfilled not going to be, but already fulfilled. And having done it, believe that all things are possible to the Lord Jesus Christ; and you just saw Jesus Christ in action, for you saw the creative power of God in action, and that's Jesus Christ. That is your own wonderful human imagination.

Now believe in the reality of what you've just done. Believe that this subjective appropriation of your objective hope for a friend is a fact. That is really praying. And all things are possible to God. Go within and appropriate it just completely appropriate it, and see it unfold within your own vast marvelous world.

So this wonderful secret is the secret of the Lord Jesus Christ. If you turn on the outside and turn to another, you do not know the Lord Jesus Christ. You can make all kinds of images of Him. That's not the Lord Jesus Christ. If any man should ever come and say, "Look, there he is," or "Here he is," don't believe it. Why? Because when you actually meet Him, you are going to meet your Self. The Christ of faith comes to us as one unknown; yet one who in some ineffable mystery lets us experience who He is; and when we experience Jesus Christ, we experience Him in the first-person, singular, present-tense experience. You will never see Him coming from without. Let no one tell you you're going to meet Him coming from without. You will meet Him awakening Himself within you as you. That's the Lord Jesus Christ. That's the great sacrifice. He is crucified on Humanity.

Every human form is the cross that He wears; and in that form He awakens as the one in whom He awakens. He awakens as that Being, and that Being is the Lord Jesus Christ. And because He is the father of David, David called that Being, "Father"; then you know, "I AM He."

Oh, I can tell you from now to the ends of time, and I may not persuade you to believe it; but when it happens to you, you need no further persuasion, for you are confronted with

The Secret Of Imagination: Imagination Fulfills Itself

the facts and there you stand in the presence of you own son, and the son is the Son of God.

"I will tell of the decree of the Lord," said David. "He said unto me, 'Thou art my son. Today I have begotten thee.'". These are the words of David in the Second Psalm. "I will tell of the decree of the Lord. He said unto me, 'Thou art my son.'" That son is going to call you, "Father"; and then, and only then, you will know you are God the Father. That is the mystery of the entire world. And so, what you accomplish in this world concerning finances is wonderful for you as an individual in the world of Caesar. What you do concerning the social world all these things it's marvelous; but you will only really fulfill your destiny as you fulfill scripture, for the purpose of life is to fulfill scripture.

"I have accomplished the work Thou gavest me to do." What work? All that the prophets spoke about me; and beginning with Moses and the prophets and the Psalms; he interpreted to them in all the scriptures the things concerning Himself. Then said he, "Scripture must be fulfilled in you," and the purpose of life is to fulfill scripture the prophecy of God to man, for He gave man Himself, or promised to give man Himself. And He promised me a son. The son He promised was His Son; and in giving me His Son, He gave me Himself, for His Son calls me, "Father." And that is the whole mystery of life. There's nothing but God. One Being expanding Himself forever and forever and forever, each Himself. And even though he calls you, "Father," may I tell you, you will not lose your identity. You are individualized and you will tend towards ever greater and greater individualization. And yet, you are the Father of my son; and if you are the Father of my son, then you and I are one. It is a great mystery, we are brothers, for you do not lose your identity and I do not lose my identity. So you and I, behind these masks are eternal brothers the Father of the One and only Begotten Son.

Well if you are the father of my son, and my own wife is the "father" of my son, then the relationship on earth of men, or friend to friend and wife to husband, is above this level, and we are eternal brothers, all forming the one Father.

So tonight, you take me seriously; and when you go home or start it here, you put into practice this greatest of all secrets; the secret of imagining. There is no greater secret in the world. Every child born of woman is alive because it was imagined. And imagining is God in action. That's the soul of man imagining; and that is the power of God. And the power of God is Christ. And that is the wisdom of God, and the wisdom of God is Christ.

A child can imagine. Well, that's Christ. That is Christ crucified on that little tiny garment, and it suffers with everything that that little child imagines, or it enjoys with everything the little child imagines. It wears all the stripes and all the blows that man in his misuse of that power will do. He doesn't criticize him. He waits upon me as indifferently and as quickly when the will in me is evil as when it is good. That way, He bears all my stripes. He bears all of my misuse of His power, knowing that in the end, I will awaken and use it only lovingly.

When I completely awaken from the dream of life, I will use this creative power of God only lovingly. But in the meantime while I am trying to awaken to the use of this power, I misuse it. And may I tell you, you will confront this vision, and you will see what you did from the beginning, for you didn't begin it a few years ago in your mother's womb. You have been coming through the centuries.

One night, here I saw this monstrous creature covered in hair. It looked like a gorilla, and the hair was all dark brown from head to toe. It was a monster. And here, the most glorious, heavenly creature a female; and this was a male monster. And it called out to this heavenly creature, "Mother, mother." Well, I knew this could not be this radiant, heavenly creature; and so I struck him. And as I struck it, it gloated; it loved violence. And I pummeled it, and it gloated all the more. Well, it could speak in a guttural tone, calling this heavenly being, "Mother." And that annoyed me. Then suddenly from within me I knew. Why, this is my own creation. And so is this one. They are only the out-picturing of my two different uses of the creative power that I AM.

Here (the monster) is the complete embodiment of every misused moment of my life. Every time I was violent, I created and fed this monster. It whispered in my ear to be monstrous, to be violent, to be bad, to be evil, for it fed only on this thought. And here (the heavenly creature) was the embodiment of all my loving thoughts. Every kind, considerate, wonderful thought in my life fed this one.

As I saw this monstrous thing and realized that it was my own offspring, it was the fruit of my misspent energy, I pledged myself. There was no one to whom I could turn, I pledged myself that if it took eternity I would redeem it. It did not come into being through any power other than my own misuse of my own power. It could not have been brought into being; and that thing could not live, and it could not help itself. I didn't condemn it.

At that moment, I felt compassion beyond the wildest dreams of anyone for this monstrous thing that I had created. And when I made myself that pledge that I would redeem it if it took me eternity, at that very moment, the whole thing got smaller and smaller and smaller; but it didn't waste the energy that it embodied returned to me. I began to feel a power that, until that moment, I had never felt before. And this one began to grow. The beauty that she embodied and personified glowed as the energy came back from this one (the monster) to me; and the whole thing dissolved before my eyes.

So, "nothing is lost in all my holy mountain" I did not lose that energy that I misplaced, it returned to me, that was embodied in that monster. And throughout the centuries, it was it who whispered in my ear monstrous things to be done, because it could only feed on violence. It could only feed on evil.

Then I realized what it meant: that I ate of the Tree of the Knowledge of Good and Evil. And so it fed upon evil, and she fed upon the good. And then the evil that was only the energy misspent returned to me; and then the whole thing came back to me. And then I broke the spell, and I awoke in this world.

Well everyone is going to confront that gorilla on the threshold. Everyone has him, unseen by mortal eye, and he whispers into your ear to entertain the unlovely thoughts of the world. And your every reaction that is unlovely, it feeds upon it; and your every thought that is kind and wonderful and loving, she feeds upon it. And the day will come, you will be strong enough to confront this. And may I tell you, it will take you the twinkling of a second to dissolve it? You don't labor upon it. All it needs is the core of integrity within you. When you pledge yourself, and no one else, you don't swear upon your mother, you don't swear upon a friend, you don't swear upon the Bible; you pledge yourself to redeem it. At the moment you pledge yourself, and within you, you know you mean it, the whole thing dissolves. It's no time at all in dissolving. And then all the energy returns to you, and you are stronger than ever before to go forward now and eat of the Tree of the Knowledge of Good and Evil.

And if you forward and misuse it again, you start another form building; and one day you will dissolve it again. Eventually you will become completely awakened, and you will use your wonderful power only not for good, that tree will come to an end, for Life itself. For eating of the Tree of the Knowledge of Good and Evil is this world. The day will come that you will eat of the Tree of Life that bears the fruit of truth and error. Error will embody itself here, and one day you will confront the error, and the error will dissolve before your mind's eye as truth begins to glow before you, because you are eating, then, of the Tree of Life as you formally ate of the Tree of the Knowledge of Good and Evil. And the combat of good and evil produces this monster, and the combat of truth and error produces an entirely different form of being, more glorious than that one of good and more horrible than this. The error will dissolve just as quickly when you confront error.

So if today your teaching is not true and you live by it, you are building something just as monstrous; but one day you will confront error and you will discover that you lived by a false concept of God something on the outside of Self; that you formerly worshiped a little golden figure made of gold and silver. It had eyes, but could not see. It had ears, but could not hear. It had a mouth, but could not speak. It had feet, and it could not walk. It made no sound within its throat. And those who made it are just like it. And those who trusted it are just like it too.

So all the little icons in the world that people worship these are the little things called "error"; and one day you will discover the true God. And when you discover the true God, you will find that He is all within your own wonderful being as your own wonderful human imagination. You'll walk in the consciousness of being God. You don't brag about it.

As Blake answered when they asked him, "What do you think of Jesus Christ?" Blake answered, "Jesus Christ is the only God"; but he hastened to add to it, "But so am I, and so are you."

So you don't tell anyone. You simply know that you are the Being spoken of in scripture as "God the Father." For all that is said of Him, you are going to experience; and you are going to experience it in the first-person, singular, and a present-tense experience. And then you will know.

Today is the eleventh year since it happened to me right here in this city, right across the way at the hotel with the star at the top of the roof, the Sir Francis Drake, on the 20th day of July 1959. It was then that I, at 4:00 in the morning, felt within my head the most intense vibration, and I thought, this is a brain hemorrhage, and this is it. I knew nothing of the human form, and I thought I cannot possible survive what I am feeling; so this must be what they call a massive brain hemorrhage. But instead of departing this world, I awoke to find myself within my own skull; and I knew that I was entombed completely within my own skull. I was fully awake, as I've never been awake before, and here I am sealed the skull is sealed, and I am in it. The skull is not a little thing like this (indicating the head). It's the size of a huge, big sepulcher, and I knew it to be my skull. I also know intuitively that I could get out by pushing the base of my skull.

As I pushed it, a stone rolled away, and I saw the little opening, and I put my head through it and pushed; and I came out, inch by inch, just as a child is born from the mother's womb. But instead of being born from below of flesh and blood, I was "born from above" out of the skull Golgotha, where Christ was buried. But it was not another coming out, I am coming out. There was no other. I had no companion in that skull. I myself was there, and I came out. And when I looked back at the body out of which I came, it was ghastly pale, turning its head from side to side like one in recovery from a great ordeal. I stood up and looked at it, and then suddenly I heard this strange, strange wind this unearthly wind that I had heard in the tomb within my head, well now, it seemed to be divided and coming from the corner of the room.

As I looked over to see if it really came from that side, and I looked back three or four seconds later the body had been removed. There is no body; but in its place sat my three older brothers. My eldest sat where the head was, my second one sat where the right foot was, and the third one sat where the left foot was; and they heart this same unearthly wind. They couldn't see me. I not only saw them, I could read their thoughts as I could read my own. Their thoughts all were objective to me. Everything was objective. They couldn't have an emotion that wasn't objective. They couldn't have a thought that wasn't objective. And yet, I heard their voices.

And then my brother Lawrence got off the bed and started towards the same direction that I thought this wind originated this peculiar wind. As he took one or two steps, he said, "Why, it's Neville's baby. This is the cause of this peculiar, unearthly wind."

My brother Victor and my brother Cecil, they said, "How can Neville have a baby?"

He didn't argue the point. He lifted from the floor a little infant wrapped in swaddling clothes and brought it and placed it on the bed; and I took that infant up into my arms, and as I looked into its face and said, "How is my sweetheart," this little heavenly face broke into the most glorious smile; and then the whole scene dissolved.

There was the resurrection from the dead, followed by the "birth from above." So we are "born from above," as told us in the Book of Peter. "We are born anew through the resurrection of Jesus Christ from the dead." (1st Peter 1:3). There is only one Being resurrected, the Being who descended into man; and that is Jesus Christ. He descended into man, the power of God and the wisdom of God, and united with man; and when they became one and fulfilled the destiny of that Being, only He now wakes as you. And so, you awake as the Lord Jesus Christ, without loss of identity.

So eleven years ago on the 20th day of July, back in 1959 here in this city, that drama took place within me. So it is my birthday today in a spiritual sense. The little body that now stands before you, that came in the year 1905. It will depart and turn into dust; but that which awoke within me is the Immortal Self that cannot die. And those who have not had the experience, that Immortal Self is still there, and it cannot die. You will be restored to life in a world just like this to continue the drama until that experience that I've just told you takes place within you.

Nothing dies. The little rose that bloomed once, blooms forever. It turns to ash as the body will turn to ash, but you the Immortal You, who is all imagination cannot die. But it will awaken one day in the same manner that it awoke within me. It was buried in Golgotha, which means "the skull." He is buried on Calvary, which is the skull. It is in the skull of man that God is buried; and there God-in-man will awake.

So here this night you put it to the test as you are challenged in scripture to test Him. And you test, not another, you test your own wonderful human imagination, for that is the Lord Jesus Christ.

The truest story ever told is the story of Jesus Christ. Let the world rise in opposition and say there is no Lord. As Blake brought out so beautifully in his poem "Jerusalem":

The Secret Of Imagination: Imagination Fulfills Itself

"... Babel mocks; saying there is no God or Son of God; That Thou, O Human Imagination, O Divine Body of the Lord Jesus Christ art all A delusion; but I know Thee, O Lord, when Thou arisest upon My weary eyes, even in this dungeon and this iron mill ... For Thou also sufferest with me, although I behold Thee not.

... And the Divine Voice answers, ... Fear not. Lo, I AM with you always, Only believe in me, that I have the power to raise from death Thy Brother who sleepeth in Albion."

You can't get away from your own imagination. You can't get away from it because that's your own being. That is the reality. But it suffers with you. He is the Lord Jesus Christ within you. Now test Him tonight. Test Him for the good. Do you want a better job when they say they are letting people out? Forget what the papers say. Forget what anything says. "All things are possible to the Lord Jesus Christ.".

If you don't have enough money, forget what the paper says, you assume that you have it. "All things are possible to God." He sets no limits whatsoever on the power of believing. Can you believe it? Well, try to believe it. Try to believe, first of all, in God. Well God is your own imagination. Well believe in Him; that whatever you can imagine is possible.

Can you imagine that you have now the kind of a job that you want? The income that would come from it? The fun in the doing of the work? Well then walk as though it were true; and to the best of your ability believe that it's true. And that assumption though denied by your senses, though the world would say it is false; if you persist in it, it will harden into fact. This is the law of your own wonderful imagining. Believe it, and it will become a reality.

Metaphysical / Law of Attraction Books

David Allen - The Power of I AM (2014), The Power of I AM - Volume 2 (2015), The Power of I AM - Volume 3 (2017)

David Allen - The Creative Power of Thought, Man's Greatest Discovery (2017)

David Allen - The Secrets, Mysteries & Powers of The Subconscious Mind (2017)

David Allen - The Money Bible - The Secrets of Attracting Prosperity (2017)

David Allen - Your Faith Is Your Fortune, Your Unlimited Power (2018)

David Allen - ASKffirmations: Questions That Create Reality

The Neville Goddard Collection (All 10 of his books plus 2 Lecture series) (2016)

Neville Goddard - Assumptions Harden Into Facts: The Book (2016)

Neville Goddard - Imagination: The Redemptive Power in Man (2016)

Neville Goddard - The World is At Your Command - The Very Best of Neville Goddard (2017)

Neville Goddard - Imagining Creates Reality - 365 Mystical Daily Quotes (2017)

Neville Goddard's Interpretation of Scripture (2018)

Neville Goddard - Consciousness, The Giver Of All Gifts (2019)

Neville Goddard - The Wish Fulfilled (2020)

Neville Goddard - The Story Of Jesus Is Persistent Assumption (2021)

Neville Goddard - The Secret of Imagination: Imagination Fulfills Itself (2021)

The Definitive Christian D. Larson Collection (6 Volumes, 30 books) (2014)

David Allen - The Within Creates The Without: Creating Our Lives By Design: Daily Meditations

David Allen - The Creative Power Of Mind: Daily Meditations For A Better Life

www.ingramcontent.com/pod-product-compliance
Lightning Source LLC
Chambersburg PA
CBHW030910080526
44589CB00010B/228